TIGER TACTICS

CEO Edition

FROM ZERO TO LAW FIRM CEO

TIGER TACTICS

CEO Edition

FROM ZERO TO LAW FIRM CEO

Jay Ruane
Ryan McKeen
Billie Tarascio
William Umansky
Elise Buie
Jennifer Gore-Cuthbert
Sandy Van

Michelle Dellino
Joey Vitale
Mario A. Godoy
Allison McKeen
Allison C. Williams
Seth J. Price

DEDICATION

*For all the lawyers out there brave
enough to be CEO*

About the Authors

Ryan McKeen

Ryan McKeen is co-founder and CEO of Connecticut Trial Firm, LLC in Glastonbury, CT. He has grown a solo practice to a team of 35 (and growing). In 2022 Connecticut Trial Firm obtained the highest jury verdict in Connecticut history - $100 million. He speaks nationally on how to grow and run a law practice and legal technology. He is a tireless advocate for a healthier legal profession. The true loves of Ryan's life are his wife Allison, his children Talia and Luke, and dogs Teddy and Masha.

Jay Ruane

Jay Ruane is the owner of Ruane Attorneys at Law LLC in Connecticut and founder of The Criminal Mastermind. In addition to his law firm and coaching, Jay also is the CEO of FirmFlex, a social media marketing platform for lawyer. Jay worked defending DUI cases for over 25 years and expanded his office to include post-conviction work. In that, Jay successfully led the exoneration litigation for 2 men now free after spending decades in jail for murders they did not commit. A frequent lecturer on law firm management, marketing and systems, Jay created the online group The Law Firm Blueprint and lives in Connecticut with his wife and law partner Jill, and his 4 children, Julianna, Robert, James, and Isabelle.

Billie Tarascio

Billie Tarascio is the owner of Modern Law, a family law firm in Phoenix, Arizona and a co-owner of Win Without Law School and Modern Law Practice. Modern Law is a six-time award winner of the law firm 500 award and a Clio Riseman Award Winner. She was also named 2019 ABA Rebel. Billie is a true entrepreneur who has been experimenting and pushing the legal model throughout her twenty-year career. Billie is one of the original authors of Tiger Tactics and the author of Decode Your Divorce 1 and 2. Billie is also a mother to four children and active in building social media communities.

William Umansky

Bill "the Lawman" Umansky is a seasoned attorney from Orlando, specializing in Personal Injury and Criminal Law. With 30 years under his belt, he now mentors lawyers aiming for seven to eight-figure revenues. Bill once presided over his local Rotary Club and founded the Second Chance of Florida scholarship foundation, promoting education for brighter futures. He's the acclaimed author of "Tiger Tactics" and host of "The Lawman's Lounge" podcast. Bill, husband to attorney Zahra and father to Zak and Jake, relishes travel, cooking, fitness, and time with dogs Boots and Bella. Rooted in the philosophy "Everyone Deserves a Second Chance," compassion drives his every move.

Joey Vitale

Joey Vitale is a trademark attorney for thriving brands. He owns Indie Law, one of the most reviewed trademark firms on Google, and he has filed over 800 trademark applications. Joey and his team help small business owners protect their brands and build the legal foundation they need to thrive. Joey has spoken to tens of thousands of people across the world, and he is sought after for podcasts, conferences, and to be featured in articles. He is also the CEO of Skybreaker, which helps online business owners build trustworthy teams so they can cut their work week in half.

Seth Price

Seth Price is a founding partner and the business backbone of Price Benowitz Accident Injury Lawyers, LLP, a Washington, DC-based law firm. Seth's commitment to creating a firm that provides excellent representation and exceptional customer service led Price Benowitz's growth from 2 attorneys to more than 40 in less than a decade, covering multiple areas of legal focus. Seth is also the founder and CEO of BluShark Digital, a best-in-class digital agency focusing on the legal sector. An accomplished attorney and transformational thought leader, Seth is often asked to speak on law firm development and legal marketing strategy and is a frequent lecturer and moderator at some of the largest and most influential law conferences in the United States.

Michelle Dellino

Michelle Dellino is CEO of Dellino Family Law Group. She is also a rescue dog mom, wife, friend, family law attorney, traveler, and baseball fanatic. Not necessarily in that order. She started her firm ten years ago based on the belief that there is a solution to every problem and a better way. Since then, DFLG has solved problems for thousands of people. Michelle makes sure her team always has the tools to take a case anywhere it needs to go and the support to get there. She holds her JD from Seattle University and MA from Arizona State University.

Allison McKeen

Allison McKeen serves as the Chief Operating Officer of Connecticut Trial Firm, LLC, where she has been instrumental in driving a tenfold increase in revenue over a five-year span. Her leadership and practical enhancements have enabled the firm to scale effectively, reflecting her unique perspective on implementing vision through constant adaptation. When not immersed in solving operational, financial, and personnel challenges, Allison indulges in her passions for beekeeping, gardening, and knitting. She resides in Connecticut with her husband Ryan, their children Talia and Luke, two dogs, bringing joy and vitality to her personal world just as she brings growth and innovation to her professional one.

Jenn Gore-Cuthbert

Jennifer Gore-Cuthbert founded Atlanta Personal Injury Law Group, a leading Georgia firm handling auto collisions, trucking incidents, slips, and wrongful deaths. Leveraging technology and superior client communication, they've built a reputation for case value optimization and legal efficiency. Established in 2013, the firm has grown remarkably in caseload, revenue, and staff. Recognitions include awards from The National Trial Lawyers, Superlawyers, and AVVO. Additionally, they ranked on Inc 5000's Fastest Growing Companies list in 2022 and 2023. Jennifer, also a national speaker on Law Business, coaches upcoming attorneys. She serves on boards for Atlanta's John Marshall Law School and the Georgia Association for Women Lawyers. A community supporter, Jennifer backs the Achieving Your Goals Scholarship and Atlanta Back Pack Project. Married with three kids, she loves fitness and travel.

Mario Godoy

Immigration Attorney Mario Godoy specializes in family-based law, citizenship, removal, and criminal defense for immigrants. Born in Guatemala, he embodies the immigrant American Dream. Arriving in the U.S. at a month old, he grew up with Spanish as his first language, speaking English only from age 6. Inspired by his parents' pursuits—his father earning a Master's and his mother starting a salon—he was driven by memories of a deported relative and family injustices. This led Mario to law school, aiming to make a change. He founded two law firms: Godoy Law Office Immigration Lawyers and Estate and Probate Legal Group. As an immigrant, husband, and father, Mario emphasizes the significance of family unity in America.

Elise Buie

Elise Buie, a Seattle-based attorney and founder of Elise Buie Family Law Group, focuses on family law and estate planning. A survivor of Hurricane Katrina, her own divorce, a relocation, and blending families with Doug and their six children (now 20-somethings). Elise knows firsthand what it means to successfully integrate lawyering, entrepreneurship and parenting while elevating into the CEO (Chief Enthusiasm Officer) roll. When not advocating for civility in divorce through a child-focused lens, you can find her hosting and mentoring young lawyer leaders while enjoying the Pacific Northwest from her oasis on the Hood Canal.

Allison Williams

Allison C. Williams is an international speaker in the field of child maltreatment, national media contributor, featured author, and a decorated trial attorney who is a Fellow of the American

Academy of Matrimonial Lawyers and chosen by her peers as one of the Top 100 Super Lawyers in New Jersey. She founded Williams Law Group, LLC, grew it from start-up to multi-million-dollar enterprise in 3.5 years, and then founded Law Firm Mentor, LLC, a business coaching service, which helps Law Firm Owners crush chaos in business and make more money. The motto of Law Firm Mentor is #NeverStopGrowing!

Sandy Van

Sandy Van is a successful entrepreneur with a multifaceted business empire having founded Van Law Firm, a legal virtual assistant administrative outsourcing agency, and is soon to be a general partner in an investment fund. She thrives in building businesses and giving back to underserved local and global communities. Her plan for the future is to be an inspirational leader showcasing success which she defines as the right balance between financial success, relationships, health, personal growth and contribution. Sandy is a philanthropist and a serial entrepreneur.

Get Exclusive Access to the Authors

INTRODUCTION

Tiger Tactics was conceived of late on a Friday night, in a group chat between Ryan McKeen, Jay Ruane, and Billie Tarascio. Now comes the follow-up book, which continues the approach from the impactful and profound original. A diverse array of highly successful lawyers was once again assembled, and this time was tasked with answering the big questions leaders of law firms eventually face. Their different, but complementary, skillsets and goals come together and build on each other in this book to paint a comprehensive landscape of the world of top lawyers.

At Fireproof, we teach the importance of clarity, alignment, and accountability to law firms. We guide law firm leadership teams through a process to gain agreement on answers to the key questions, including who, what, when, where, why, and how. We gained firsthand experience with growing our business by a factor of ten in ten years, as we built Mike Morse Law Firm into a nine-figure firm, and we have coached hundreds of firms of varying shapes and sizes at almost every stage. We understand how difficult it is to build a healthy, thriving law firm. This is why I especially appreciate the valuable insights shared by the authors as they tackled huge topics, such as The Transition to CEO, The People You Will Need, The Tools You Will Need, The Challenges You Will Face, and The Vision Forward. This book would have been extremely helpful to us during the early phases of our growth, in particular. It will deliver great insights to any law firm owner or leadership team member, regardless of practice area, size, or location.

I'm blessed to know a great majority of the authors personally; I have appeared on their various podcasts and serve as a business coach to several. I respect each of them and the different paths they have chosen. I have no doubt that you will choose your own path, as well, making decisions that are unique to your goals, time, and place. The messages that resonated with me when I read the book will, in all likelihood, be different from the ones that connect with you in that moment. As you transition to becoming a seven-figure firm - and then for some an eight-figure firm – the points that stick out to you will probably evolve as well. Tiger Tactics CEO Edition will have something to offer you no matter what stage your firm is at in its growth. These are very individual questions, and the authors hold nothing back in their answers. Their authenticity and vulnerability are remarkable. They share their insights from their own experiences and are paying forward the lessons learned from both their successes and failures.

Lawyers are trained to be story tellers. I find the choice to share these origin stories in parable format to be engaging and makes the information accessible to those unfamiliar with the business world. Importantly, these lessons are shared in the authors' own voices. You get the real deal, the intimate answers usually reserved for a close friend or respected colleague. I loved seeing their personalities on full display, lots of lessons in that, as well.

The questions are purposeful and focused. They are centered on helping successful founders of law firms navigate the tricky evolution to CEO of a business. Whether you are beginning your transformation, or are well into your journey, I cannot imagine a better use of time than learning from others who are where you want to be.

I implore you to dive into this book and extract all the wisdom it has to offer. It will help you shape your plan of attack, save you precious time, and help you attain the lifestyle you desire. There's even a big reveal at the end, which I won't spoil.

I'm so proud of my friends for creating and sharing this book with us!

John Nachazel

Cofounder of Fireproof

October 2023

TABLE OF CONTENTS

CHAPTER 1

The Transition to CEO

Ryan McKeen

There's no easy part to any of this. None.

Becoming a lawyer is hard. Being a lawyer is hard. Starting a law firm is hard. Growing your law firm to a million in revenue is hard. Every step on the journey is harder than the next.

Transitioning to CEO reminds me of the transition I made from couch potato to marathoner. One day I laced up my running shoes and went for a run. My sole goal was to get in better shape. That run turned into doing a 5k, and then a half marathon, and then a marathon.

Becoming a marathoner requires one thing above all else. It requires that you want to run a marathon. It is that simple. If you want it enough you find your training plan, invest in necessary gear, you hit those eighteen mile training runs in the heat or sleet, and during the race when it really hurts—you push through. It's impossible to finish a marathon without wanting to finish a marathon. The distance is too long and the race is too hard if you don't really want it.

The same can be said for becoming a CEO of your law firm. The price of admission is wanting to become the CEO of your law firm.

It's my goal in this chapter and the ones that follow to walk you through my journey. To tell my story in as accurate of a way as I can in hopes it connects with you. Wherever you are on your journey. There is no one way to do this. The goal of this book is that you get enough perspectives from people who have done this that it puts the wind at your back along your journey.

Whether you are thinking about opening your own firm, you are solo, or you are a lawyer with a few employees, the first alligator that you have to wrestle with is vision.

First: What Do You Want for Your Firm?

Becoming a CEO means that your firm operates like a business. One can be wildly successful and profitable as a lawyer with a few paralegals and maybe an associate.

If you want to be a CEO it means that you have to build a business. It means your days will look very different. You will be removing yourself from the delivery of services. And instead focus on leading others who deliver those services.

In order to do this it requires that you make a choice to grow your firm. You will have to invest in marketing that drives growth. You will have to invest in systems that sustain growth. And you will have to attract people who can do things better than you can do them.

You will have to get comfortable with big numbers. Your monthly overhead in a few years may be a multiple of your current salary.

If you want your firm to operate like a business—keep reading.

First: What Do You Want for Yourself?

Becoming a CEO requires you to want to exclusively work on your business.

The transition doesn't happen overnight. It's not the kind of thing where one day you are in court all of the time and the next you are working on your business full-time. Much the same way you don't go from couch to the finish line of a marathon in one day.

Transitions always feel weird to me. It is the space between where I am and where I want to be. It is uncomfortable. You will have to get used to letting go of where you were and relentlessly pushing forward to where you want to be.

If you want to lead a business—keep reading.

My Journey

I have done it all.

I started as a solo and languished for many years. I would make money but it was never enough to hire someone.

I flipped that switch and grew a small firm. And then the small firm kept getting bigger and bigger.

I know the pain points well. There isn't enough time or money in the very long days it takes to scale a firm.

I have worn too many hats for too many days.

The Thing You Must Do

I'm not a *must* or *have to* kind of guy. There are many ways to do or succeed at anything. Some great business people get up at 4 a.m. and have a routine that works for them while others sleep in. The challenge in most things is to find the thing that works for you.

Transitioning from wherever you are on your journey to truly being the CEO of your business requires one thing—letting go.

In many cases your firm may be founded on your reputation as a great lawyer. That is why your phone rings. That is why others want to work with you.

If you are to be a CEO it isn't about being a great lawyer. It is about making the lawyers around you into better lawyers.

For that matter it is about making everyone and everything your firm does better.

The job for any leader is to create space—for team members, for great work to happen, and for systems to be built.

The CEO of a law firm is the producer of the movie and not the star of it.

You must be willing to make this transition. Your success will largely depend on the success of those around you.

It is your job to find people capable of succeeding and put them in positions to succeed. That means your focus is to get them the work they need, the tools they need, the money they need, and supply them with the vision that only you can.

You will have to stop doing a lot of things in order to focus on the important things.

Your new job if you want it involves vision, rallying others to your vision, constantly searching for opportunities, threat identification, coaching, and solving all of the most difficult problems your organization faces.

Jay Ruane

I guess you can say I was one of the luckier ones among our tribe. I knew what solo and small firm life was like before I entered it because I grew up with it. My father is an attorney, and when I was growing up he worked as an associate at a law firm. I saw how hard he worked, even when his name wasn't on the door, but I also saw how it impacted him when his boss fired him during my freshman year of college because he wanted to save the salary for himself.

So he hung a shingle, much like many of us and created a job for himself. He never really approached law as a business. If you read the first Tiger Tactics book, you know I tell our firm story, and part of my personal journey was recognizing that he truly wanted no part in being a business owner, it was thrust upon him. But I was different. Having worked at another competing law firm, I saw inefficiencies in how they did things, and also where I could make changes, if I only had the power. I think for me my own journey to CEO started long before law and is just part of who I am. I was never going to be a good and dutiful employee. I believed in myself (maybe too much sometimes) and wanted to chart my own course, so when I joined with my father, an unspoken division of labor occurred, which eventually became more formalized, then got me to the CEO role I am in today.

I remember the early days well. When I finally admitted out loud I didn't have the passion for the profession that he did, it was like a weight was being lifted, but I needed to make myself useful. I wanted a challenge, and I wanted to feel fulfilled, and building a firm felt like something I could tackle and win at. So I brought it up to my father slowly over our lunches.

I explained I didn't find joy in doing the trial work like he did. He countered that I could never run a firm without such experience to be able to manage hundreds of cases simultaneously. He was right to some degree, but I knew that even modest simple business practices would do wonders for our firm, and I set out to learn as much as I could.

This wasn't as easy as it is now. Trust me, I know it is not easy now too, but it was much harder when there were no podcasts or seminars for entrepreneurial lawyers. But I started spending time looking for books on business in the local bookstore, and picking up magazines weekly to see how other businesses functioned. Even though the lawyer related content was minimal, I could find corollaries in other service based businesses, so I set out to just read as much as I could. When I found an author that made sense, I devoured anything else by them I could. When a magazine had a great idea, I would tear it out, so I could refer to it again. Over time I built up some knowledge and would apply it to our firm, trying ever so slowly to create simple processes and plans to make our practices systemized. This wasn't to scale necessarily. This was to avoid the work I hated for the most part. And that is where a lot of my systems started. If I hated (or strongly disliked) something, I wanted to create a system to get through it as fast as possible or delegate it to someone else. I guess I was "lazy" like that. I wanted to AVOID work.

So soon enough I was looking for ways to scale and bring in other attorneys who could execute so that I could avoid those things I hated and it forced me to truly embrace the CEO role and start thinking about both day-to-day operations and long-term strategy, two things that probably 99 percent of lawyers (the ones not reading this book) never consider.

For me the CEO role was really my attempt at minimizing my workload. I wasn't necessarily right about that, but I have found I can focus more on the things I love as CEO.

My own transition to CEO started once I knew I had attorneys who could do all the routine court appearances, leaving me for the more complicated matters. Then I realized that the complicated matters were better handled by someone else. I think part of being a CEO is not falling into the ego trap, or at least being aware of the ego trap. You'd like to think that nobody can do anything better than you at your firm, but the truth is, there are a lot of people who will be better at you at many things, but nobody can see the great vision and moves you need to make to execute as CEO. We are not your standard lawyers who think of our role as mitigating risk. Our job is to embrace risk and take chances, and once you get that mindset shift, you can really do wonderful things as a CEO.

So I slowly moved items off my plate to people who do it better. And through that process I came to learn that knowing enough about a topic to make educated decisions is a key skill of any CEO. You have to be able to take in information, assess and interpret it, then make the call. Undoubtedly you will flub a few calls, but there is almost nothing you can't come back from as long as you maintain composure and integrity.

One of the most interesting things to me as I developed into the CEO, I actually started finding some small joys in representing people that I never had before. So now, as CEO, I can delegate some of that work I like to myself, and be useful to the team as a pressure relief valve if needed. The transition to CEO and filling this core function is perhaps even more lonely than being a solo lawyer just scraping by, because when you are a solo, if you have contact with other solos, you develop a kinship with others going through the same struggles. But there are even fewer lawyer entrepreneur CEOs out there in the world, and you have to be comfortable with the choice you make. Luckily my coauthors in this book have helped me through some tough times. Find your group, either locally or online. It will make your world infinitely better.

Hugh MacLeod, a British artist, has some artwork that has resonated with me ever since I started on this journey and I bought it for the wall behind my chair in my office. On the artwork it says "The price for being a wolf is loneliness, the price for being a sheep is boredom. Choose one or the other with great care" and I truly believe in that. Not all are cut out for this life as a CEO, but if you are, there is no other path.

I've been willing to embrace the CEO role because it allows me to be my authentic self. I take risks, I embrace change, and I want to be a giver and employ people and give them a home. It's become my calling, and it took a while to get here and understand that, but once I did, the sky was the limit.

Billie Tarascio

There wasn't a moment I transitioned to CEO. I was always a CEO and the iterations of CEO have occurred many times over in my now 17-year career as an attorney. My early years as CEO felt more volatile. There was a steep learning curve and the kind of flexibility that exists when you don't have enormous payroll obligations each month. There was a big learning curve to understand domains, building websites, opening bank accounts, choosing office space and hiring people for the first time. Each of us will bring to this role unique gifts and great instincts for some aspects of business and other aspects where we are woefully inept, destined to repeat a version of the same mistake what feels like a million times. As a CEO you must have a high tolerance for risk and you must be willing to accept a huge amount of responsibility. If you have those two things and a love for business, the best you can do is the best you can while enjoying the ride.

My career began with a baby born my third year in law school in 2004. I knew I wanted to practice family law and began working as a contract attorney for as many lawyers as I could. There were two firms/lawyers that I worked with for several years and I volunteered. I met with people who needed legal help and found that many people could afford some help, but not $250/hour help. As a new attorney, with no overhead, there was no reason to charge $250/hour. If I could make $50-$100 per hour that was more than I had ever made waiting tables through college. So, I dabbled. It was low pressure.

My church sent clients and many I met with for pro bono help hired me. I had a small and successful solo practice. It was fun, but I was always an entrepreneur and fascinated by the business model of lawyers. There had to be a way to offer services to middle and low-income clients. I didn't understand why legal services had to cost so much.

I learned about limited scope legal services and built a business plan based on high volume and low-cost services. I moved to Arizona in 2009 where there were unemployed lawyers everywhere. Arizona and Oregon had just opened admission by reciprocity after five years of practice. I decided to wait on taking the bar and hire other lawyers to execute my business plan. I took my plan and projections to NEDCO, the neighborhood economic development commission. If I opened in a low-income area, they would give me a loan. I launched this far-fetched, never tried business model without a license to practice law in Arizona. Looking back this was such a naive move- so many of them were.

Nevertheless, I persisted. The local papers ran articles about my $99/hour, pay as you go, limited scope business model. The company made $150,000 in gross revenue and saw just under 1000 clients. My projections of filling the day with clients who came in for document review or consulting all day long were not a reality. Clients wanted representation, not just coaching. The economics didn't work, because I didn't have the volume I needed. I also didn't have the budget to make the volume work. The model needed to change. The Company needed a CEO.

Fast forward to the end of 2022 and Modern Law looks like a lot like a more traditional firm. We practice only family law, have 11 lawyers and thirty-three full-time employees. I know I am the CEO because the practice of law has never been my sole or even primary focus. The practice of law was always a piece of my role but never the most important. My most important role has always been protecting the organization and I have failed more times than I can count.

For those of us who are entrepreneurial at heart, things just grow. They continually expand. To date, there are five related but separate companies to Modern Law. The first sister company was created in 2013, I Do Over. I couldn't transition away from low-income assistance into being a traditional and expensive law firm without figuring out a way to serve the population I had committed to serving. I Do Over is a legal document preparation company that offers low-cost legal document preparation. We can offer flat fee divorces, without lawyers, for $1299.

Next came Modern Law Practice, a consulting company for lawyers. My passion for the business of law has been seeping out for decades and I have spoken all over the country and the world about business models, key performance indicators (KPIs), law firm culture, marketing and intake. My partner Chad Burton and I own Modern Law Practice and work with law firms to provide outsourced intake, law firm dashboards of KPIs, marketing, tech, and other operational support.

Two of the LLCs are office buildings I bought and operate Modern Law Offices out of. Those are pretty simple and have provided outstanding tax benefits to me as the owner of the firm.

The final and newest LLC is called Win Without Law School. This company is owned by me and my partner Julie LaBenz. We offer live and online courses for people representing themselves and newly licensed legal paraprofessionals in Arizona. This course provides education to give people trial skills. It teachers how to operate in court or prepare for negotiation. It teaches people how to tell their story and organize facts and evidence. It is the most comprehensive resource for self-represented family law litigants in the country and can be found at winwithoutlawschool.com.

While my path has been straight and narrow, always an entrepreneur and always a CEO, it has not been smooth. My biggest struggle has been management. As a CEO you depend on others to execute your vision and make good on the promises you make to the public in your marketing. And your team depends on you to provide them structure, clarity, and the resources they need to do their job well. I have struggled to transition from a scrappy clan culture to a larger team that requires more structure and uniform accountability. I have underestimated the amount of administrative support it takes for a team of thirty-three employees and 300 annual clients to function well. I have consistently made bad hiring choices and bad firing choices.

Bill Umansky

I distinctly remember the moment I transitioned to CEO of my law firm, albeit not a good one. You see, I'd been in practice on my own for about four years. I had a case manager, a paralegal, a legal assistant, a receptionist, and some interns. We were killing it! My reputation as a criminal lawyer in Orlando grew, and the cases were coming in fast and furious. Case volume and money were not a problem. I thought about hiring another lawyer but could not bring myself to do so for fear that nobody else would care about my clients like I do. I micromanaged everything, including how my case manager and litigation paralegal, both with more than twenty years of experience, would work on files and draft litigation pleadings. The same approach bled into the way I would hover over how our books were kept. I delegated nothing and stressed about every detail of my law firm. Frankly, the person I micromanaged the worst was myself. I dared not delegate anything to anyone if it required my intelligence, wisdom, or experience. Clearly, I had a huge ego, and the person I was hardest on was myself.

In the rare event I did not win a hearing, motion, or trial, I second-guessed every decision leading up to the ruling. If I assigned a task and a mistake was made, I would immediately regret my decision because I erroneously perceived that those mistakes would put my reputation at risk. For example: If an employee misspelled a client's name on a pleading, I would get angry and "just do it myself." I ranted, raved, and browbeat my team, and it was all just a clusterfuck.

I was overwhelmed, overworked, and just about to throw my hands up in the air. I didn't know if I could ever grow the firm, and I was too afraid to hire any lawyer. That all changed when I finally decided to hire another lawyer. I was lucky, because no one out in the market was good enough (stupid, right?), but I had someone in my back pocket. She was an experienced ex–public defender who handled large cases, a former city prosecutor and legal adviser. She was tough, smart, and very aggressive. My first hire was my wife, attorney Zahra Umansky!

That first step toward letting go marked the genesis of my transition to CEO. I still had to accept the fact that to be a CEO you need to delegate and trust the people around you. Although I thought I could do that with my wife, I realized I didn't trust her, either! As you can imagine, that didn't go over well, but there was a pivotal moment in our work relationship that transitioned me into a real CEO! Abject fear!

As you can now guess, I started micromanaging her. One day ,I was watching her handle a case in court in a way that was not to my satisfaction. I thought I would have handled it completely differently. After court was over and the client left, I approached my wife. I went on paternalistically and condescendingly to explain to her how to handle her case! My wife lifted that regal head of hers and looked me deadpan in the eyes and said, "Go fuck yourself." She went on, "You are not going to micromanage me like you do with your team. You keep doing this and you are going to end up a lonely and miserable human. You will never delegate or grow, but you will end up in the early grave." She turned her high heels and stormed off.

Man! I was so pissed off, the heat of her truth red on my face. As tempers cooled and I started thinking about it, I realized that ultimately, she was right. To run a law firm, be less stressed, and begin to scale, I would have to let go and begin to delegate, even though people would still make mistakes and perhaps not live up to the standard I set for myself.

That was my starting point to transition to CEO. I began to treat my team better, read books on executive management and leadership, and most of all, I was less hard on myself. From experience, I would tell you that if you are ready to transform from lawyer or owner of your firm, you must let go of your ego and your demons and trust other people. You must hire competent and intelligent individuals and let them do what you pay them to do. A great CEO has the ability to lead from behind and trust his team, knowing that in the end, you will live a better life if you don't browbeat everyone—including you!

Joey Vitale

When I look back on my journey as the CEO of my law firm, I see it as having three acts.

Act I: From Oddball to Rock Star

During my first few years out of law school, I worked at a highly respected firm in my hometown of St. Louis. My parents were proud that I was a lawyer—the first in the family—and the firm had a solid reputation. Plus, given the state of the economy at the time, I was grateful to have a job that paid well.

But there was one big problem. As hard as I tried, I just couldn't seem to fit in. I felt like the ugly duckling most days at the office. I'm a natural peacemaker who doesn't like to argue. The confrontation in the courtroom and in depositions made me stressed and nervous. Plus, I had a background in social media, graphic design, and blogging. I'm pretty creative, and this firm was more traditional and didn't care much for marketing or innovating.

Even the fact that I went by "Joey" instead of "Joe" was a point of contention and a bit of a joke with some of my colleagues. "Come on," someone told me during a work lunch. "Do you really think a client would rather hire a 'Joey' than a 'Joe'?"

I was having an identity crisis. Could I really be myself—a "Joey"—and a good lawyer? Should I even *be* a lawyer?

After two years of working on my weaknesses, I finally mustered the courage to have a hard conversation with the managing partner and put in my notice. I'd taken a massive leap, and I had no idea where I'd land.

Let's fast forward to a few months later. With the help of some great mentors, I decided to start my own firm and help emerging businesses. And as I started working directly with entrepreneurs and small business owners, I noticed something magical happening.

Everything that made me feel "less than" at my old firm ... my peacemaker attitude, my positivity, my creativity, my interest in marketing ... it all gave me superpowers in this new niche. Even going by "Joey" was a breath of fresh air for these clients. It turned out they craved someone approachable, kind, and unintimidating. In fact, I quickly grew a Facebook group to over five thousand entrepreneurs who sought my guidance for keeping their businesses protected.

The Takeaway: Find your "oddball edge," the unique traits you possess that might be deemed a weakness unless channeled in the right direction. We all have extraordinary greatness inside of us, and we have a duty (to others and to ourselves) to unleash it.

Act II: From Lawyer to Entrepreneur

My first year as a law firm owner was exhilarating. At my old firm, there were layers of attorneys between me and the clients. Now, for the first time, I was in direct contact with clients—all of my clients. While there were stressful days, I found it addicting in the best way. I loved hopping on calls with clients and feeling their rush of relief and understanding after I clarified how trademark laws work.

But it was also my first-ever experience as a business owner. And while I certainly felt a responsibility toward my clients, I also had this huge responsibility to my firm. How would I keep clients coming in?

I quickly realized I had to see myself as a business owner more than a lawyer. I started hiring local and overseas teammates to support me so I could focus on the other parts of the business. I spent more and more time reading business books, creating content, having sales calls, managing finances, attending conferences, and creating processes. It didn't take long for me to understand that, as much as I enjoyed working with my clients, my time was better spent elsewhere.

The Takeaway: As a law firm owner, your time is now even more valuable. Your time is better spent building and growing the business than doing all the legal work.

Act III: From Entrepreneur to CEO

I hustled my way to $100k my first year, which at the time was beyond what I thought was possible for myself. But it also put me in the hospital for two weeks.

Shortly after my one-year business anniversary, I found myself up past midnight, freaking out about work. The stress wasn't new, but this time felt different. I couldn't breathe. It literally felt like the world was ending. I didn't know it at the time, but I was suffering from a panic attack.

At the hospital, it got even worse. Despite the extra medications doctors gave me, I kept having panic attacks. Each one seemed more severe than the last. My family feared the worst, as there were signs that pointed to possible brain damage with severe long-term effects.

I won't lie. I was scared for my life. But I was equally scared for my firm and my clients. What would happen if I couldn't complete the client work on my plate? While I had a small team around me, so much of the firm's success still relied on me.

Luckily for me, this story has a happy ending. Eventually, the doctors discovered that I have a rare reaction to most anti-anxiety medications. Once they changed up my medication, I made a quick recovery.

On my last day of outpatient care, one of my primary doctors pulled me aside. She said, "We're confident you'll be just fine. But your brain just went through a very traumatic experience, and it will take a while to rewire itself. Over these next few months, you have to do everything you can to create a stress-free law firm. Doctor's orders."

Looking back, I am thankful for that wake-up call. That experience started a three-year journey where I built a strong leadership team around me. Quarter by quarter, I let go of more roles in the company. Today, I only spend about two hours a week working inside my firm.

The Takeaway: The more your business depends on you, the less it is worth. The time you spend designing yourself out of every position but CEO is the highest-value use of your time—for your own health and for the health of your business.

Seth Price

The transition to CEO is one of the greatest challenges a lawyer faces when building their law firm. Between Price Benowitz and BluShark Digital, I've had the privilege of seeing hundreds of law firms from the inside, revealing common patterns in what entrepreneurial lawyers struggle with when building their practices. What distinguishes those who succeed is that they've recognized a critical need in structuring their firm: a CEO.

There are countless components to building a law firm, and although every part plays a role in the final construction, not every role is created equal. It's important to focus on different parts at different stages of the journey; as your firm scales and grows, your priorities should adapt. For example, many people begin their law firms with a focus on producing legal work. Before they transition into CEO roles, many law firm owners are all about the hustle—more business, more cases, more clients, and more staff. Of course, this is absolutely necessary to get a law firm off the ground—but what happens as the workload increases? The firm grows, new employees join the team, and suddenly the person who used to manage it all is in over their head. Their focus must shift beyond just legal work.

At a certain point—ideally, as early in the process as possible—leadership must take hold to manage the many moving parts necessary for the firm to grow and succeed. The transition to CEO holds practical and theoretical importance in a law firm's evolution. In practice, the questions you ask yourself at the beginning of each day may shift from "What work needs to be done?" to "What people and resources do I have in place to take us to the next level?" On a more theoretical level, your perception and scope in managing your law firm must grow to not only meet your goals but exceed them and anticipate the next ones.

Imagine a game of chess Like an experienced chess player, a CEO can take a step back and figure out their moves a couple of turns ahead rather than simply reacting as challenges and opportunities arise. Without a CEO role, you may be taking pawns today when you could be setting yourself up for checkmate in the future. You need someone with the perspective to look at the landscape ahead, and you need the bandwidth to allow them to focus on the future. Without the personnel necessary to cover essential operations, a CEO in name cannot function as a CEO in practice.

The CEO role requires multiple skill sets in planning, supervising, and conducting quality control. For instance, one of a CEO's many responsibilities is to oversee the division of the law firm as it is built out across different departments beyond just legal production—intake, accounting, marketing, etc. Early in a firm's growth stages, a CEO must bring these people together. Over time, a COO will take on some of these responsibilities, allowing the CEO to inhabit their role in its purest form: someone who works on their business rather than in their business. A great CEO can leverage their integration skills to create harmony within their firm just as readily as they can apply that expertise to a wider scope.

When you're working to unite people to achieve a common vision, you need a certain level of social intelligence. This requires knowing when to brush things off and when to double down, when to be resilient and when to cut your losses. There are countless decisions involved in running a business that are entirely circumstantial—there is no formula or rulebook for finding the right answer. As an entrepreneur, you get used to people fighting to keep you from building something meaningful. You have to learn to tune out the noise and keep the ball moving for you and your team. This is the only way to build and expand in your role as CEO.

It's important to remember that these functions aren't taught at law school. Some of the best CEOs are born to lead, and the rest learn the necessary skills through experience, courses, and trial and error. Master classes are invaluable opportunities for lawyers—or any new entrepreneurs—looking to transition into a CEO role.

Mentor figures are another resource many legal entrepreneurs may overlook. The idea of a leader as a lone wolf can only stunt your growth and limit the potential of your firm. There is always someone who can teach you something, and those who build their support networks and tap into those social resources are the ones who will come out ahead. Find the people in your field you admire, the ones who are where you want to be, and seek their mentorship. More often than not, they will remember the mentors who helped them along the way and be happy to pay it forward.

Above all, I truly believe that it is the CEO's desire to lead that determines whether a law firm will make it to the highest level. From the beginning, a true leader must ask themselves what they need and what needs to get done to allow them to inhabit their role as CEO. There are so many different roles in a law firm. Depending on your practice's stage of growth, many of those components might be missing. In the early days, part of a CEO's job is to help steer the ship and make up for missing hands on deck. As those openings are filled, the CEO steps away, allowing their team to flourish while they focus on bigger operations and systems. While law firm operations are always critical, they can also be outsourced.

As a CEO, you must allow yourself to take the helm as a visionary and leader for your firm to reach its highest potential. A firm needs someone to focus on leading the team to ever-higher stages, just as it needs people to focus on marketing, intake, legal work, and any number of other essential tasks. Affirming your commitment to transitioning into the CEO role is the first step in a series of challenges you will face.

Allison McKeen

Entrepreneurs have a special place in my heart. My grandfather opened a small pharmacy in the 1950s after he graduated from school. It had a soda fountain and everything—very Norman Rockwell. He supported his family with this business and even opened a second location, eventually hiring three of his four adult sons. My dad worked there for most of his professional life. I also had my first job there.

Southwood Pharmacy was located in the middle of a network of neighborhoods and easily accessible by foot for the many families that did not have two cars. We sold diapers and greeting cards, penny candies and school supplies. It filled a need in the community, and although the pharmacy supported Little League teams and school fundraisers, we didn't have to advertise. Instead, the focus was always on service. We filled prescriptions on holidays and delivered to those who were homebound. When my grandfather passed away, friends shared memories of the pharmacy and the various, quiet kindnesses he'd shown them. This business was an opportunity for him to give back.

But behind the scenes, it wasn't all rosy. Holiday dinners were often overshadowed by heated discussions and unspoken resentments. Everyone was doing too much, and yet some things were not getting done at all. Scheduling shifts was messy, payroll was run late at night, and I don't know who was responsible for mopping the floors or organizing the back storage room. Yes, the business was running, but no one was really leading it. And when a buyer presented a generous offer in the late 90's, no one had the vision to see that the landscape was changing. Families no longer walked to the pharmacy for emergency items. Worse, some insurance companies stopped working with us, mandating their insureds use big chains. My family declined the purchase offer only to be forced to close the business years later.

It's easy to get caught up in the day-to-day when a business is young. When opening a law firm, you do everything, by necessity. You run marketing, counsel clients, and run accounts receivable. The focus is on producing something that consumers want, so you direct your energy toward that product. The actual business side of a new law firm is relatively modest.

But as your firm grows, it takes on a life of its own. Hiring employees solves some problems while creating others. Suddenly you have a group of people who need to be paid, trained, managed, and provided with benefits. You may need office space, computers, and a pantry stocked with snacks. Now that you have a team to bring your legal services to a larger market, you have more clients. Are they all getting the same level of service that your early clients did? How do you know? And now that your law firm is supporting so many families, how will you guarantee its continued success in a rapidly changing market?

There comes a point at which the business becomes a demanding beast that needs constant, consistent attention. If you don't feel this shift in your gut, you'll certainly feel it in sleepless nights and grueling weekends spent trying to catch up. You may wonder if any of this is worth it. You want your life back—should you return to collecting a paycheck?

I know this pain, and I've felt it deeply. My husband Ryan and I went all in on Connecticut Trial Firm in 2018. There was no second job, no safety net. We had two young children who were depending on us and a mountain of debt. When the business of our law firm grew into a dragon, we had two options: lead it, or walk away. Continuing on the current, unpredictable path was not an option.

During this time I thought of Southwood Pharmacy and how it served the community but not its owners. I didn't want the same for our family. I wanted to have a business that allowed us space for other things that mattered outside of work. We chose to lead our law firm by transitioning Ryan into a CEO role.

If you're struggling to manage your firm, you're not alone. Lawyers—like others who sell professional services—are especially resistant to thinking of their firm as a business like any other. But if they don't turn their attention at some point to the business itself, they will find themselves living and working in chaos. Our family pharmacy was missing a CEO: a person who served the business rather than directly serving its customers. We needed someone to be thinking two steps ahead instead of reacting to whatever came in the door. We needed systems and rules, not hastily scribbled signs reminding us not to chew gum. While the rest of us were caught up in managing the day-to-day, we needed someone to see the opportunities—or lack thereof— on the horizon.

Having a monopoly on legal services ensured law firm success in the past, but the practice of law is changing. Between the internet, artificial intelligence, and private equity entering the market, lawyers don't own the market any more. It's not enough to bill accurately and do good legal work and trust that clients will always need your services. Clients have other options now, and they will only hire you if you provide the right customer experience.

The CEO is the person who decides what that customer experience needs to be, from intake to resolution. This is the person who sets the tone and vision for the firm and puts it in the best position to compete in a changing landscape. If the CEO is doing their job well, profit and security will follow.

The transition from business owner to CEO isn't an easy one, but we're going to give you some guidance on how to do it. Running your law firm like a business will not only set you apart from the competition, it will improve other aspects of your life. If you are carrying anxiety with you, I promise that once you become the leader your business needs, you will breathe easier.

Michele Dellino

Your transition to CEO of your firm does not have to look like everyone else's journey. There is no right or wrong way to make the transition. You might be there without even realizing it, and simply need to solidify your focus on what you need to do to be successful in the role. Or you may be completely entrenched in the legal work in your firm, have no management structure or systems in place, and need to start from ground zero. Most people are somewhere in between.

Whether you are beginning in the transition or solidifying it, having a roadmap for what you want your role as CEO to look like is smart planning. I did not do this until later in the game, but I recommend you do it early on. Create a living, breathing plan you can adapt and work from while you grow and lead the firm. You can't get to the CEO role or do well in it without knowing where you are going. Giving yourself some benchmarks and direction for your role and the pieces you need in place will help you plan ahead so you can pull together the people and the tools you'll need to be ready to deal with future challenges.

I have always had a mind for business, so part of my brain has always been in the CEO role, even when I was deep in the legal work. I always wanted "out" of the legal work to fully live my purpose as CEO. I held a very clear vision for myself that required gradual extrication from the level of legal work I was doing, delegating the things that did not need to be on my plate, and, most importantly, identifying the things I love to do and where to spend my energy as CEO.

When I identified what I wanted my CEO seat to look like, I had to stop comparing myself to other people. It is important that you have a community of other law firm CEOs so you have people to bounce ideas with and learn from, but you do not have to do everything they do or do it the same way.

Some people will tell you that you should stop doing any legal work. Initially, that was my goal. But when I was honest with myself, I realized that, although I don't want to be a full-time litigator anymore (and I do not have time for it as CEO), I actually do want to have the flexibility to maintain a small number of cases and projects, keeping my foot in the legal work as much or as little as I want. I love what I do as CEO, but I am lucky to be a lawyer and a very good one, so leaving room on my plate to take on a case or project that speaks to me is a dream come true. I can take a case because I want to, not because I have to. This has let me do things like co-counsel a civil suit for victims of sex trafficking and work with a handful of family law clients whose cases resonate with me.

That is something I never would have had the time or energy to do before, let alone felt it was okay for me to do as a CEO of my firm. I have learned that if I am intentional with my time and goals, I can do whatever I want to do so long as I set limits for myself and am disciplined with my time. I cannot take five cases, but I can take one or two I really want to take at any given time. If you do not still love practicing law, you should stop. You, as CEO, do not have to do it anymore, and there are plenty of other places to spend your time in the firm. If you do love it—or if you are just really competitive like I am—leave room on your plate for it while setting limits.

Shaping myself as the CEO of DFLG over the past several years has been personally and professionally empowering. Allowing myself to own the visionary role on my team as CEO is beneficial for both me and my firm. I truly wish the same for you.

Allison Williams

I often marvel at the number of attorneys who hate being lawyers. That was never my story. I loved lawyering from the moment I found it. When I was at a firm that required 2000 billable hours per year, I gladly billed 2400. Workaholism is a real thing, but so is the pursuit of excellence. And I achieved mastery much earlier than my peers because I was fanatical about work.

Unfortunately, that method of attaining career success does not carry over to being a business owner— but in my ignorance, I tried. Sixty-hour work weeks became seventy, which became eighty. I "tapped out" at ninety. And because I had not mastered the art of hiring people, I was several months in, having fired my third legal secretary, and finally simply opted to do it all myself.

The result? At the end of one of my ninety-hour work weeks, I collapsed under the weight of exhaustion, fell asleep while driving, and woke up 1/4 centimeter away from the guard rail.

"Jesus, take the wheel!" was a very real circumstance in my life, and quite literally saved my life. Thankfully, the near-death experience woke me up to my natural talent for systematizing everything. I applied the chaos-crushing framework that I now teach to thousands of lawyers in my coaching business, Law Firm Mentor, and I started to come up for air.

If You're in, I'm Out!

Massive change began when I started hiring lawyers. My first critical mistake was hiring the cheapest talent I could (i.e., a "baby" lawyer). My young associate was hungry to learn, but I needed more help than her limited experience could offer. I needed another version of me in order to transition my clients without complaint.

By the time I started a law firm, I had a statewide litigation practice. Most attorneys handle child abuse cases by taking court-appointed work at a low hourly rate; I charged my full $500 hourly rate. I tried cases in all nineteen counties in New Jersey, taught judges and lawyers regularly, and created a blog (before blogging was "a thing") that was cited by several media outlets. I had been interviewed countless times as an authority, lectured internationally, and appeared on the Katie Couric show to address the issue of false allegations of abuse in families.

So when my clients would say, "I don't want to work with anyone else; you're the juice," it was pretty easy to buy that story, let it feed my ego, and let it keep me trapped in lawyering, unable to get to the stuff of building a business.

But I did it. I escaped the courtroom so I could build my business, and by doing so, I exponentially increased the number of families that could benefit from my expertise. That is why I vociferously disagree when lawyers insist that they are too special, too notorious, too whatever to convince their clients to work with a member of the team. Without any egotism in this statement, I give it to you with certainty: if I can do it, you can do it too.

But how can you move your clients to a member of your team? First, you can't simply walk your client down the hallway, hand them over to another attorney, tell them they are in good hands, and think they will believe you. You have to be strategic.

Your law firm marketing and branding must speak about your team, your process, your documented "special sauce." If you sell "you" on a platter, that is what people will buy, and they will feel deprived if they don't get you.

Second, you have to ease your way out of existing cases. Add a second attorney to the file and make them the bigger voice in the room, the more available person to take phone calls, the one who starts to handle issues in the file. Often, clients need to see it to believe it, so give them firsthand experience of your employees' expertise to create buy-in. Then, you can be unavailable, and the client will not mind.

Third, you need a person trained in sales to conduct your consultations. If you are a big name and you handle the consultation, your client will be unhappy when you are not the face of the file. That person can be an attorney or a non-attorney.

Finally, every part of your firm process must include the expectation that you are not the face of a file. That includes your intake department, your legal sales team, and other attorneys on the team. If you choose to be involved, that is your choice; it should not be your shackle.

Trusting Others—Is This a $500 Per Hour Question?

A major impediment to business building is the persistent interruption. Your team will face decision fatigue. You must train them well but still expect that they will make mistakes. Checks and balances baked into your systems prevent those mistakes from being catastrophic.

Avoid the "open door" policy that invites people to bother you whenever. I used to ask my team, "Is this a $500-per-hour question?" when they interrupted me. That might sound off-putting, but it reminded them that every interruption costs the firm some portion of my hourly rate for the time it takes me to answer.

That said, you must be available to your team until you are no longer needed. Do this by creating an "open floor" policy. This means regularly schedule meetings. Issues arising between these meetings are addressed in "office hours," i.e., blocks of time scheduled throughout the week when you are available for "quick questions." As you systematize your firm, your office hours become less necessary.

You will never become unnecessary to your law firm until you decide to be, communicate to everyone that you are the last resort, and reiterate that their success in your firm depends upon their ability to be resourceful at all times and to solve their own problems.

Jenn Gore-Cuthbert

As someone who opened their own law firm immediately after getting their license, transitioning from being a law firm owner to a CEO was relatively simple for me in some respects. However, I did face several significant challenges. Growing up in an entrepreneurial family where my dad had various businesses, and studying business in college, I always knew that I wanted to own my own business. But in law school, I was told that law firms were not really businesses but "professions," which left me feeling confused.

Becoming a CEO

Becoming a CEO means running your law firm like a business. I always knew I was the business owner, but I struggled with where to spend my time when I first opened the law firm. I was wearing so many hats and scrambling to keep all the balls in the air. I did not feel very much like a CEO.

At the beginning of my journey, I faced a tough decision: should I focus on becoming the best lawyer possible, or should I dedicate my time to developing the skills necessary to become a successful law firm business owner, capable of leading and managing a team of talented lawyers? Despite my love for practicing law, I recognized that if I were the sole provider of legal services in my firm, its potential for growth would be very limited. It became clear to me that my time would be better spent running the company, and that if I were to focus solely on legal work, my freedom to manage and grow the firm would be greatly restricted.

As I made the transition to CEO, I realized that I had to let go of my identity as the one who solely performed the work and embrace my new responsibility of delegating tasks to the appropriate individuals. It can be easy for your ego to convince you that you are the only one capable of doing certain tasks, but this is simply not true. It was important for me to establish a new identity as the CEO to successfully make this transition.

Running the Law Firm Like a Business

To run a law firm like a business, you need to have a thorough understanding of all the major functions within the firm, including marketing, intake, legal production, financials, software/technology, people, and facilities. This approach requires developing a budget and a strategic plan, making informed decisions based on data, hiring the right people, and staying focused on the big picture. It involves spending more time working on the business than the legal work. Delegating work and finding talented individuals to replace you may be difficult initially, but it's necessary for the long-term success and profitability of the firm.

Getting Coaches

One thing that ignited my transition to CEO and running the law firm like a business was my exposure to law firm business coaches very early on. At year two of opening up my law firm, I met several people in Atlanta who were working with business coaches for law firms and experiencing success. I saw their firms growing and hiring new staff in a short period of time. My initial thought was, "Why on earth would I need a business coach? I am from a family of businesspeople, and I went to business school!" But as time wore on, I quickly recognized that working one-on-one with a coach had clear advantages.

What I quickly discovered during my transition to CEO and running my law firm like a business was that the lessons I learned in business school were not enough to prepare me for the unique challenges I was facing. That's why I decided to attend my first law firm business conference in Miami and signed up for coaching on the spot. This decision marked the beginning of my journey in finding and hiring coaches and mentors. By learning from successful law firm owners with larger firms than mine, I was able to triple my law firm's revenue in just one year. I was like a sponge, absorbing as much knowledge as possible and constantly asking questions. What was particularly helpful was that many of these business owners were from outside my state and were more than willing to share their experiences, struggles, mistakes, and setbacks. In contrast, back in Georgia, it often felt like people were guarded and only shared information selectively.

Data

You cannot be a CEO if you don't have a handle on your law firm data. The beginning stage of data is just starting to collect data. This process can be super simple. I began by just writing things down, creating Excel spreadsheets. You should at a minimum know:

- How many potential clients call you
- How many clients you sign up each month
- Your conversion rate
- The known source of each potential client and client
- Which marketing activities bring in most leads
- Your average case value for recovery and attorney's fees
- How much legal work needs to be produced each month
- The biggest bottlenecks to your cash flow?

The next phase is looking at the data you've collected and making hypothetical guesses as to what your benchmarks should be. You begin to use data to plan and execute. You will have to make a hypothesis for:

- How many cases should you be signing up per month?
- Which marketing activities should you do more or less of?
- How much legal production needs to occur monthly, quarterly, annually?

- o How many lawsuits need to be filed?
- o How many demands need to be sent?
- o How many settlements need to occur?

Finally, you will need to get good at reviewing, analyzing, evaluating data, and expanding your data. You will learn to look for patterns and data points, cyclical trends and key indicators.

- At what time of year do we see typically lower lead volume?
- What can we do to get ahead of that trend?
- If we increase these marketing activities and get more cases, how much sooner do we need to hire and increase staff capacity to service those cases?
- What is the capacity of each of my legal teams?
- What cases bring in the most revenue and why?
- How can I get more higher-value cases?

Too many law firms use data as a historical record of what already happened in their firm. I use data as a dashboard like driving a car in real time every day.

- Do we need to accelerate the gas?
  - o Do we need to ramp up marketing?
  - o Do we need to ramp production?
- Do we need to put on the brakes?
  - o Do we need to dial back a marketing channel that's broken?
  - o Do we need to dial back legal production until we fill vacant seats?
  - o Do we need to hire more people because we don't have enough capacity?

When a data points starts dropping or ramping up, you should immediately dig in and see what is causing the change and to troubleshoot the problem. But you can only have this kind of control if you have data in real time that is easily digestible and makes things easy to understand.

Elise Buie

Be honest with yourself—do you have what it takes to be the CEO of your law firm? Here are some factors to consider.. The CEO role may not be for you if:

- You are a hot mess who can barely lead yourself, much less others
- You can't handle the truth – think *A Few Good Men*
- You have money mindset Issues
- You absolutely love practicing law
- You have not read and have zero interest in reading 1000+ business/self-improvement books
- The Mean Girl in your head (mine is named Eloise) is downright verbally abusive
- You think 2400 billable hours per year sounds difficult (ha ha—try 5000 hours per year)
- You value your freedom—you *might* stay out of jail, but that is about the extent of your "freedom"
- You have no experience in failing, let alone regular, large, public failings
- Managing people is a drain on your soul no matter how hard you try to get it right
- You thought *The Devil Wears Prada* was a powerful example of good leadership
- You hate change
- You are conflict-avoidant
- You lack radical candor
- You are a people-pleaser
- You like being right
- You want to do everything yourself
- You want to be the smartest person in the room
- You want to watch TV or scroll on social media in your spare time

- You don't enjoy difficult conversations
- Risk scares you
- You want consistent sleep each night

If, after reading this list, you still think it is a good idea to lead your own law firm, buckle up, brace yourself, educate yourself, and enjoy the wild ride. I am not normally a Debbie Downer, but the reality is that this CEO role has challenged me more than anything I have done in my entire life (including raising a brood of children through many difficulties, including Hurricane Katrina and divorce—four bio children and two bonus daughters). The CEO role has been utterly exhilarating and unbelievably exhausting. If you know my story, it's clear that I do not shy away from chaos or obstacles. A few highlights of the chaos through the years: becoming the caretaker of my mom and her parents during law school due to strokes within months of each other; evacuating my lifelong home in New Orleans because of Hurricane Katrina; helping one of my BFFs and her six children relocate to Texas in the aftermath of Hurricane Katrina, then coping with her untimely cancer death; evacuating to Georgia, then to Minnesota; my own divorce after an infamous email from my ex days before I took the Minnesota Bar Exam, which sent me to the ER for a suspected heart attack; homeschooling four children, an Offer in Compromise with the IRS during my Hurricane Katrina evacuation; three cross-country moves in the wake of Katrina along with two bar exams, remarriage to the amazing Doug Russell, two stepdaughters, and my middle son's life-altering car accident in high school. None of this, however, prepared me for the ups and downs of the CEO role.

Let's step back a bit. I started Elise Buie Family Law Group, PLLC virtually in February 2015 solely to pay for my kids' education. At that time, we had kids in elementary school, middle school, high school, and college. Some years we paid more than $250,000 in education costs between private schools and college. My entire focus was earning enough money to pay the tuition bills each semester. I focused on the grind rather than on developing a strong business with a strategic operational system. Those lack of systems would later cause much upheaval when we were in a fast growth mode.

The one system that we mastered early on, due to a medically emergent maternity leave, was that of Clio, our practice management system. We were diligent about adding everything to Clio and ensuring that each matter had current notes and up-to-date tasks so that anyone in the office could pick up a matter and keep the case moving forward. We have thought of Clio as our "shared brain." Our Clio system was tested in a medical emergency when our most experienced attorney was severely injured in a horseback riding accident. This solidified by love affair with Clio hygiene. In our firm, we consider good Clio hygiene to be part of self-care, team care, and client care.

My transition from grinder to "CEO" officially began on February 29, 2020 when Covid reared its ugly head in Seattle—the initial epicenter of the Covid 19 pandemic. On that leap day, my son, who had spent the previous night at a friend's house, reported that he might have been exposed to Covid from his friend's stepdad, who treated those first Covid patients. On that same day, we watched Washington's Governor Inslee announce the first US Covid death, right here in Seattle. Also on that day, my daughter called to report that she lost her job on the Buttigieg presidential campaign as he was midflight en route to Notre Dame withdrawing from the presidential election. February 29th was also my stepdaughter's birthday. I immediately told my team (six people at the time) that we must stay away from our office and warned them that their kids' schools would be closing imminently for several weeks. They thought I was melodramatic, yet in hindsight, of course, my estimates were significantly understated. Also on this day, I realized that I had to make some quick, strategic decisions in order to keep the firm afloat.

Immediately, I focused on the firm's survival and my team's employment in light of this abrupt shift in business and looming court closures. The firm had minimal cash reserves (up until this point, I spent everything earned paying for my kids' education costs), yet three new hires were starting on March 9, 2020. So I used my go-to problem-solving method — white boards and dry erase markers. I ran the numbers every which way imaginable. In fact, I ran forty-three different scenarios in order to figure out how I could retain my team (including the three new hires) and bring in the needed work to support all of us while the courts shut down. Around this same time, I discovered

Fireproof: A Five-Step Model to Take Your Law Firm from Unpredictable to Wildly Profitable, written by Mike Morse and John Nachazel, and read it cover-to-cover in one sitting. Wow, *Fireproof* spoke to me on so many levels. Initially, it spurred me on to bring my team together and let them know that I had devised a plan that would support their employment through the uncertainty of Covid. That plan was for me to do each and every consult that came into our office in order to convert as many clients as possible but also to provide a needed community service during this time of fear and unknowns. I spent 10+ hours each day for months doing consults and ended up converting so many cases that we needed to hire more and more people in order to meet our demands. That rapid hiring continued through 2020 and 2021.

One of my first hires in 2020 was a fractional COO type, someone who had expertise in writing systems, developing workflows, and maximizing tech integration. She was a jack-of-all-trades and helped me as I transitioned to CEO. At this point in the hiring, I knew nothing about culture and did not have firm core values. We did not have job descriptions. We were hiring quickly to keep up with the demands of the new cases. (The problems associated with this fast growth are discussed in a later chapter).

We started working with the Fireproof team, who helped us implement the Entrepreneurial Operating System (EOS) system into our firm. Fireproof and EOS changed the way that I thought about Elise Buie Family Law and my CEO role. I set off on a mission to build a team around me to do all the things that I should not be doing—because I was incompetent at them (i.e., writing systems), because those tasks were not worth my hourly rate, or because I wanted to work less than 100 hours per week. To this day, I continue to identify tasks that I should not be doing. A CEO's role is often best limited to a few things: numbers, people, culture, and big relationships.

Every insecurity and mean-girl thought shouted by Eloise, my resident "mean girl," has surfaced during my tenure as CEO. Forget run-of-the-mill mean girl thoughts such as "You are not good enough." Eloise goes for my jugular, thoughts like "You are a bully for holding someone accountable," "You deserve to have people issues because you are a bad person," "You don't deserve financial security because you are bad with money," and "Only greedy people focus on productivity and cash flow." The list of Eloise's abusive comments is long and memorable. I have battled Eloise each and every day of this CEO adventure. After spending more than $100,000 on coaches and therapists since 2015 and reading endlessly (often 100+ books per year) about personal development and leadership, I am now equipped to eavesdrop on Eloise, question the veracity of what she says, and push back. I no longer blindly believe Eloise's abusive comments.

As Seth Godin says, "Time to dance with the fear." As entrepreneurs, we are growing our visions out in public. What is visible and in use is five to ten percent (maybe) of our real vision. It is scary to put it out there in its incomplete form with the warts and all as we continue to build, making improvements on ourselves and our firms each and every day. Running a business is like juggling chainsaws while riding a unicycle on a tightrope. It is a vulnerable position to be in publicly.

Due to the extensive personal development, I am now, finally, in a position where I regularly show up with the lowest heart rate in the room—a longtime leadership goal of mine. That low heart rate, coupled with high EQ, is what allows me to address the endless stream of CEO s@@@ calmly now. Doug and I have joked for years that I am going to write the "You Can't Make This Shit Up" book. Though it has been a long, arduous, expensive road to wrangle my hot-mess mindset, that personal development work is, by far, the best time and money I have ever spent. I can now address problems from a place of curiosity and with a growth mindset, knowing that my own blind spots are likely at the core of many issues. I realize that the vulnerability of what we are doing is also our superpower; it is transformational to be authentically vulnerable while you are evolving as a CEO.

Sandy Van

Transitioning to become a CEO is a journey that requires patience and persistence. It's not something that can be achieved overnight; it takes a lot of trial and error. However, you should not let setbacks discourage you from pursuing your goal. As the saying goes, "There is no manual for raising children;" the same applies to starting a law firm. Success is not a straight line to the top but rather a set of zigzags. There will be occasions where you will want to give up, close your firm, and start over from scratch. As someone who has been there, trust me, there are still days that I feel like this.

But what does being a CEO actually mean? Many attorneys are focused on working in the business rather than on the business. They are technicians who draft motions, attend hearings, tinker with their case management system, negotiate settlements, and more. But instead of engaging in tasks with a set output value of $25 to $500/hour, CEOs should focus on handling significant and crucial responsibilities, the operations for which require skills unique to you. Those game-changers include networking to learn how to do things more efficiently and even networking on deals or referrals that increase your firm's revenue. Networking is also crucial because it informs you of the next up-and-coming area of law to capitalize on. You might decide to add a new area of law to your practice or to cut dead weight in your firm. Importantly, these efforts can also lead to learning about the next technological advancement that can reduce the time or effort required to complete tasks, such as artificial intelligence, new software, or automation.

Many attorneys waste valuable time on tasks with minimal monetary reward. When one could spend an hour and make

$1,000, why spend an hour on something that could be done for $30? Getting groceries, booking travel, and running to get the dry cleaning...—when your income reaches a certain threshold, it doesn't make sense to do these things yourself. To a CEO, time is money, and such tasks are better be delegated to others, such as an assistant. Furthermore, doing mundane tasks may deplete your energy and cognitive load and cause decision fatigue. To maximize your impact on your business, free yourself from these basic chores to focus your time and attention on tasks with the highest financial returns.

Core Values

Creating a successful and efficient organization requires a foundation built on core values. These values act as an internal compass that direct a person's or organization's decisions. By defining the core values of your business, you will be able to hire, fire, and delegate based on those principles, ultimately creating a more cohesive and successful organization. They allow people in your organization to make good decisions on their own by simply applying the values to new challenges that come along. By aligning everyone in the organization with the same values, bottlenecks are removed and individual growth is encouraged.

However, core values alone are not enough. My firm measures everything by key metrics. What gets measured gets done. Everyone in my organization has a number or key productivity indicator (KPI). These metrics allow for fair comparisons to be made between team members in similar positions. This creates a sense of transparency, clarity, commitment, and teamwork. When everyone is working toward the same goal, it incentivizes successful behavior and friendly competition.

By using metrics, the organization is better equipped to determine whether they are on track to hit their annual goals and to solve problems faster if they arise. This level of data-driven decision-making is key to creating a repeatable, scalable system that ensures success.

Delegation

A team always outperforms an individual. As a CEO, you should first start building out your "A" team so that you can start delegating some of the things that you are doing, not doing, don't like to do, or shouldn't be doing. The "A" team concept is discussed in further detail below in Chapter 2:—The Challenges You Will Face. I also recommend reading *Who Not How: The Formula to Achieve Bigger Goals Through Accelerating Teamwork* by Dan Sullivan and Dr. Benjamin Hardy. It's a great book about delegation. Sometimes there are things sitting on my to-do list that are not getting the attention they deserve——like writing this book. My thought process is asking myself, "Who in my business has the skill set to draft or edit this?" The law clerks. Sometimes they have downtime. They may not create the final product, but they can start a basic draft. Once I identify and find the right people, there shouldn't be much left for me to do other than edit and give final approval.

As a CEO, it's crucial to find "A players" who can become managers and help lead the team. But these people are hard to come by, and in my experience, only 5-10 percent of employees have the skills required for this role. When putting your team together, you should trust—but verify. As Sam Walton said, "You've got to give folks responsibility, you've got to trust them, and then you have got to check on them."

Mario Godoy

I'm an immigrant, and my parents are immigrants. I thank my parents for my entrepreneurial spirit.

Growing up, I was constantly surrounded by my parents' entrepreneurial spirit and drive. My dad went to school in the United States and was an engineer and professor, and my mom was an entrepreneur with her own hair salon. I will always be grateful to them for instilling in me the importance of hard work and ambition. Growing up my parents repeatedly told me that school was my number one job. They also wanted to teach me how to manage money. In the nineties I was given an allowance of $3.00 a week. This was just enough to go out once with my friends.

From a young age, I had to learn how to make money if I wanted something nice. I had to hustle. When I wanted to buy Teenage Mutant NinjaTurtles action figures, I found a cooler and sold pop in front of my mom's salon. Whether by delivering pizzas or working in a bar or sweeping the floor, I always found ways to get what I wanted.

My early experiences gave me the confidence that I could make money and bring value to whatever venture I was working on. I watched my dad get his master's as an engineer and saw how he moved up in his company, but I also saw how layoffs were always a fear looming overhead. This wasn't just a fear my dad had—it was a fear the whole family and I experienced: If Dad loses his job, what will happen to our family?

This pushed me to want to control of my own destiny—to be the master of my own ship.

Entrepreneurship is part of my DNA.—I never worked as a lawyer for someone else; when I got my law degree, I opened my own firm. I didn't want to ever work for someone else.

In Demand but Out of Time

I made every mistake an entrepreneur can make, but I kept going. From 2011-2017, I built a practice with myself as the attorney, and eventually, I was in demand, but out of time. I was burning the candle at both ends.

Eventually, I figured I needed to find someone who could give me the guidebook on how to run a business, not just be a lawyer. I was a lawyer—but my business was running me, and my family. I discovered How To Manage a Small Law Firm (HTM) and met my first business coach, RJon Robins. HTM coaches focus on various parts of the business and guide me on managing my law firm. I also work with Kristen David of Upleveling Your Business on specific projects that we are building out.

People often ask me why I have more than one business coach. In my mind, even Michael Jordan—the best basketball player on earth—had multiple coaches through his career. When it comes to performing at your best, I believe it takes a village.

Transition from Entrepreneur to CEO

By listening and learning, I figured out how to transition from an entrepreneur to CEO of my law firm—and my life.

I realized I was managing my law firm's team the wrong way by not standardizing how we delivered legal services. Inspired by *The E-Myth* by Michael Gerber, I decided my law firm needed to run on systems. And I needed people to run those systems.

Once I made this decision to systemize our firm, I took our team to Portillo's Restaurant for lunch. For those not familiar with it, Portillo's is one of Chicago's biggest hot dog restaurants. They are very systemized in how they deliver food to the customer.

Once we got to Portillo's, I put our order in with the cashier and asked my staff to watch what happened. As soon as I placed the order, everyone at the different stations knew what to do. That's how I communicated to our staff that we needed processes and procedures to run the business. People would run the systems, but there was freedom so one person could step out and another could keep it running.

Transitioning from a lawyer to CEO happened when I realized I needed to run the law firm with systems and that my law firm shouldn't be running me.

HTM taught me how to understand the Seven working parts of a law firm:

1. Marketing
2. Sales
3. Production/factory
4. People
5. The physical plant
6. Financial controls
7. And me, the firm's owner: My goals as the owner— professional, personal and financial

I look at it this way:

I can be the owner/chef of an awesome restaurant with limited capacity because I am doing everything.

I can be the owner of the restaurant that feeds many more people because I have delegated or outsourced many functions. I can choose to be the chef myself or to hire a person who loves being a chef. But the important thing to keep in mind is that in this system, I can't be both the chef and the owner. I just don't have the time to do both jobs justice.

My CEO Mindset: Captain of My Ship

As a CEO, I had to understand and quantify my goals, and determine where I can be the most effective. Do I want to be the star attorney, or do I want run a legal business where I help more clients, my team, my family—myself?

Now as CEO, I look at Godoy Law Office and ask, *How many people can we help?*

Not what do I personally need to do—how can I help my team help more clients? As CEO, how can I help my team improve their skills and develop their professional careers so they can help our clients and our staff and clients can achieve their goals?

As CEO of Godoy Law Office, I set our firm's goal to help 1,000,000 immigrants make America their home.

I took what I learned building Godoy Law Office, and when we opened Estate and Probate Legal Group, I was the owner—not the lawyer—of the firm.

CHAPTER 2

The Challenges You Will Face

Allison McKeen

In this book about CEOs, written (mostly) by CEOs, I'm going to say something radical: You may not actually be a CEO.

No judgment—I'm not a CEO either. Lots of business owners aren't, and that's perfectly fine. There is a reason that corporate boards contain executives with diverse backgrounds and very different skill sets. The very first challenge you will face is to determine who your CEO should be.

When our leadership team began seriously considering a more formal corporate structure, we each took an in-depth personality test and met with a consultant. We'd long used personality testing in our hiring process, and we were nervous about what our own tests would reveal. But we decided that if we wanted to grow the firm in the right way, we needed to understand ourselves and each other. We also needed to establish clearly defined roles to avoid unnecessary conflict or power struggles.

At that time, our leadership team consisted of Ryan, Andrew, and me. Ryan is a visionary who loves to talk ideas in a forward-facing way (no surprise to those who know him). Andrew is a systems, rule-based type who thrives as a trial lawyer. I am a practical-minded, behind-the-scenes person who is primarily motivated to get things done. It turns out that we were a well-balanced team with complementary strengths and weaknesses. Not surprisingly, our strengths aligned with our personal interests. So Ryan became our CEO, I became COO (chief operating officer), and Andrew became chief legal officer.

You could take a personality test, but you may instinctively know where you fall. A CEO is the ideas person. They are constantly looking toward the horizon and thinking about what comes next. They come to a meeting with solutions to problems that the rest of us didn't even realize existed. These are amazing strengths. But they are also the people who are most likely to be so caught up in the future that they neglect the present. They may have trouble determining which of their ideas is best. They may not know how much money is in their bank account or what bills are due, and that's why they need to surround themselves with people who can execute and support their vision (more on that in a later chapter).

Here's a real-life example of an interaction between me and Ryan, pre–personality testing. See if you can spot the CEO.

Ryan: Let's buy a two-ton Army truck. I just saw one for sale on Facebook. We can wrap it in the firm's logo and take the depreciation this year. And we can drive it in parades or even to court, and everyone will notice it and they'll be talking about our firm a lot. Everyone will love that.

Me: Uh huh. Where are we parking this Army truck? And how will we make payroll after we buy it?

Ryan:
End scene. We didn't get the truck. I may be a wet blanket, but at least we made payroll.

Owning a business is ultimately about moving into your highest and best work life. So if you're not the CEO, that's fine. You just need to figure out who is.

But let's assume you are indeed a visionary whose talents are best used in the CEO role. As a business owner, you're probably doing things that you're not good at because they have to be done. You'll need to develop a plan to ditch those responsibilities so that you can focus on setting the firm's future.

To do this, first pause to take inventory of the job duties in your firm. What are the functions that your firm performs, and who does what? Make a list of everyone in your firm and start fleshing out their responsibilities. We call these "job buckets." Once you're finished, take a look at your job bucket. Are you filing mail? Answering phones? Formatting pleadings? Managing a heavy case load? Everything that is not a CEO function needs to go to someone else.

Why do this? Well, assign yourself a billable hour value. You don't need to literally be billing hours, but you absolutely need to value your own time in terms of what you bring to your business. Go on gut feeling, that's fine. Let's say you decide your work day is worth $200 an hour. Each eight-hour work day is potentially worth $1600 to your business. Every time you spend an hour on a task that can be done for less than $200, you are depriving your business of profit. Your business is losing $180 an hour each time you perform duties worth $20 an hour.

If you're worried about hiring the $20-an-hour employee, trust me: the math works.

So what are CEO functions? Leadership and inspiration. Vision and long-term planning. Team-building. Networking. If a different job function lights you up inside and doesn't detract too much your leadership responsibilities, then go ahead and keep it. But someone else should be ordering office supplies.

One challenge during this transition is time. You will need to assign your non-CEO responsibilities to someone else, whether that's a member of your current team or a new hire. Finding and training the right person requires time. Another challenge is money, not only because hiring someone adds to your overhead, but because you have to keep the firm running while planning your transition. It will feel like a lot some days, and you will feel like you're working too hard in order to let go.

And this brings me to the final challenge: letting go. In order to have the life you want, you will have to trust others to perform the tasks you've been handling. Transitioning to CEO may mean that you are stepping into a role that is less comfortable. Even if you've been working in chaos, that disorder may feel comfortable. So find the people you can trust when the time comes to let go, and then leave them alone. No one wants to be micromanaged.

Considering this move all at once can be overwhelming. Break up the transition into smaller, quarterly goals to make it more manageable, and set your hiring priorities. It's generally easier to find a receptionist than it is to find a highly skilled attorney, so fill the receptionist position first to buy you more time to locate the right attorney. I'm going to be speaking more about this in my next chapters.

Transitioning our CEO into his new position has taken us over a year. Part of the delay has been due to our unique circumstances and luck, but I think this is something that will simply take time. For us, it's been worth it. Even with significantly higher overhead, we've seen an increase in profits as we moved the right people into the right roles.

Sandy Van

Bad hires: I have had the misfortune to hire narcissists, sociopaths, and people who stole cases. At times I have gone above and beyond for employees, only for them to stab me in the back. Understand that you can't make everyone happy. Regardless of what you do, not all people are going to like you. Darren Hardy, editor of *Success* magazine, once talked about the important lessons he learned from witnessing President Obama's historic victory in the 2012 election. President Obama won the popular vote by 51.1 percent, but that meant that 48.9 percent didn't like him.

As a CEO, it can be difficult to find others who understand the unique challenges you face. During the pandemic, when everyone else was concerned with the latest murder mystery, I was trying to save people's jobs. It can be helpful to connect with other business owners to discuss professional and personal issues that are unique to owning a business. Becoming a member of network organizations such as the Entrepreneurs' Organization (EO) or the Young Presidents' Organization (YPO) offers an opportunity to connect and collaborate with fellow CEOs and business owners. Through this, CEOs can gain fresh insights into running their businesses by drawing upon the experiences and knowledge of others.

Are you great at hiring? If not, don't be alarmed—it's a learned skill, not an innate trait. When Van Law Firm was first starting out, I hadn't developed these skills yet, and those bad eggs rolled in. Since running a law firm doesn't come with a manual, I wrote one. I stopped what we were currently doing, sat down and read some books, and created my own process for hiring. Is this process perfect? Definitely not. However, I have greatly improved my ability to identify people who won't fit into the business's culture before we hire them and let go of those who aren't right for the business.

Whenever I've had to fire, coach out, or reduce someone's role, I've always regretted not taking action sooner. It's important to take a step back and evaluate the people around you. If you see people making a lot of mistakes or not meeting your expectations, you need to do something about it. I've never regretted firing someone; in fact, getting rid of a toxic or unproductive employee can bring a sense of relief and reduce stress for everyone on the team.

Find your "A" players. In his book, *Who: The A Method for Hiring*, Geoff Smart defines an "A Player" as "a candidate who has at least a 90 percent chance of achieving a set of outcomes that only the top 10 percent of possible candidates could achieve." In other words, an "A Player" is a candidate who stands out and has a strong likelihood of producing extraordinary results. Smart found that the worst hires can cost you fifteen times the employee's salary in lost productivity. I've had attorneys cost me millions, if not tens of millions, in settlements. You should not hire people who do not encompass your core values. Are your employees hard-working and loyal to your company?

Defining your law firm's core values and mission will help you exclude applicants who aren't a good fit and find people who are. Be willing to ask hard questions during the hiring process and weed out unqualified applicants right away. Shape your company by creating a culture that aligns with your vision.

Conduct regular audits of new hires every thirty days to assess their progress. In my company, we use internal auditors to keep track of how tasks are done, if cases are being worked on, and whether everyone is fulfilling their responsibilities. Avoid costly mistakes by identifying and removing problem employees quickly.

As your company expands, you will discover that competitors are not your allies. They actively want to see you fail. Rather than feeling discouraged and quitting, I use their hostility as a source of motivation to outperform them. Don't be put off if your rivals resort to slander or treat you unfairly; it's part of the game. Instead of allowing my negative opinions of other plaintiff attorneys in the field of personal injury to bring me down, I use that energy to surpass them and become more financially successful.

Other people can and will steal your ideas. Don't share all of your secrets! I have had competitors say to my face that an idea of mine was stupid, then turn around and copy me. For example, one of my subsidiary companies is Legal Support Help. At Legal Support Help, we find, vet, and train virtual assistants from across the globe for law firms (and other businesses) to hire as independent contractors. This could be for a short period of time, a specific project where you need more hands on deck, or maybe just to fill the gaps with administrative tasks. However, when I started Legal Support Help, no one else was providing a similar service in the legal space, and now legal virtual assistant companies are everywhere.

Seth Price

The challenges your firm will face along the journey are numerous and ever-changing, as each stage brings a specific set of obstacles.

When you're just getting out of the gate, your first tasks are fairly straightforward: form an organization, bring some business in the door, produce legal work, and get paid for it. Over time, the next challenge is to scale, allowing someone else to do that legal work. Often—and this is a hard pill to swallow—the person taking over that role will not be as good as you, at least in the short term. Over time, however, and with the multiple layers of management you will then be able to provide, that person will grow and improve in their role. All because you allowed yourself to step back for the greater good of scaling.

Letting go of perfection and control over your firm's work is no easy task, but it is necessary to achieve greater things down the road. One of my friends and mentors puts it this way: to scale, you must get comfortable with mediocrity. While I hate that fact (as I suspect many other lawyer-CEOs do, too), I know it's true. There is a precarious balance between allowing something below your best and allowing something unacceptable. That struggle is constant, real, and reemergent throughout your growth.

Let's get into the practicalities of hiring the right people to do this acceptable, hopefully ever-improving work. As you slot employees into different positions, there will be the question of quality control in hiring, training, and figuring out exactly what you need in each role. I often refer to the "rule of three when hiring." The first and second people you hire are likely wrong for the role; it may take three hires before you find the right combination of skill sets for your needs. Like Goldilocks, you need to find the middle ground between many considerations. For example, someone too senior may be bored in a role, whereas someone too junior can't meet your standard of work.

One of the challenges I've had in this position is recognizing that you won't be able to get everything right on the first try. You can't always predict how a person will fit into a role until they are actually doing it, and it may take several months to figure these things out. We've had hires who looked good on paper but were unable to meet the standards required for the position. You will also need to identify new standards as your firm grows and scales. Many firms will have at least one person who is substantially overpaid for the market. You must reassess the norms for your firm at each stage of your growth to ensure you have the people and skill sets necessary to reach the next stage.

At each stage of hiring, your organization will have different needs. Likewise, as your organization evolves and establishes itself, you will be able to attract better talent. In the early days of Price Benowitz, we made compromises in quality for our first hires. The work was coming in quickly, and we had no choice but to fill the gaps. In the next phase, we were able to hire better people who helped elevate us past the point of getting off the ground. One standout hire was able to take on numerous roles across the young organization, building a portfolio that included everything other than legal work, marketing, and intake. Several years later, when she left for law school, we started the hiring process for her replacement. It wasn't until we had hired not one but two people that we realized we actually needed four new employees to cover everything she had been doing.

Take this as a cautionary tale: when you meet rock stars along the way, incentivize them to stay. Hold on to them for dear life. When these people move to other companies, the gaping holes they leave behind cannot be easily or quickly filled. Gaining a rock star employee is a huge win in the early stages of your organization, when your goal in hiring may be to simply keep up with the demands of a burgeoning legal firm. Your next challenge is to retain those employees and continue to build a supportive structure with other outstanding hires. Building out your systems and procedures ahead of time will help soften the blow of a crucial member leaving your team.

Legacy issues pose another challenge to scaling law firms. At the beginning of your firm, everyone knows everyone. When there's a problem, someone pops in to alert you. As you scale, adding multiple levels of managers and creating layers of communication, you won't know people quite as well as you once did. It takes effort to scale while maintaining touch points of meaningful communication and preserving the workplace culture across different departments and employee levels.

However, there are also certain benefits to having multiple levels of communication in your firm. Despite the energy and enthusiasm I feel as an excitable CEO, I am no longer twenty-five years old; a younger, newer employee may feel more comfortable with a buffer between them and me, someone who can also help preserve messaging across our generational gaps in communication. As the nexus of your organization grows, these buffers are critical in ensuring everyone hears and understands your vision.

Communication and legacy issues are, at their core, personnel challenges like those you will face in hiring. Of course, there will be problems beyond the interpersonal: technology, marketing, and even physical space all pose their own challenges. As someone who has built a firm of over forty lawyers, I look back fondly on those early days and initial obstacles, but I also know there were times of deep uncertainty when I didn't know what would come next. When you build and grow with a great team and a unified vision, the path to overcoming each obstacle is streamlined. Although it's necessary to experience the struggles at each stage in the journey, you can often expedite the learning process by joining coaching groups or talking to others who have gone through similar challenges. There are tools all around you to help get your practice to the next level—all it takes is a discerning eye to identify them.

Elise Buie

Fast Growth Problems

- CEO still learning and getting in the way/flying an airplane that you are building while on fire
- Leadership does not have the needed business acumen or leadership training if brought up through the ranks
- Cash flow issues
- Systems and infrastructure not strong enough, creating people issues
- Bad culture fits—people issues—need way more HR/legal
- Not enough training/onboarding for new team members
- Your leadership needs to evolve—the people who get you to 1 mil and 2 mil, is not the same people who get your firm to 5 mil, 7 mil, 10 mil—you need strategic partners (fractional)
- Insurance—What is EPLI? Key person? General liability? Disability? Parental leave?
- Diluted customer service
- Core value misalignment
- Getting your numbers right—profit first and forecasting

This chapter is the hardest to write. I have procrastinated until just hours before the due date to tackle this one. It brings up so many issues for me as I continue to grapple with challenges and the feelings of failure those challenges trigger.

As I have stated in other chapters, we grew rapidly and haphazardly in 2020 and 2021 without many of the needed systems in place. And I ignored my own voice and concerns when bringing on our first leadership team—I wanted to bring on one person at a time, ending with the number two in command (COO or Integrator) over a two-year period, but my team voted that we do it all at once. I decided to go with the groupthink on this one despite my reservations. In hindsight, my reservations were well-founded, and ignoring my concerns caused a kerfuffle. That is one thing you can count on in this CEO role:constant failing, kerfuffles and learning. But, as one who is focused on a growth mindset, I see the lessons from this mistake, and I am grateful for the mistakes, as we all have improved because of them.

One of my lessons learned is just how much leadership training is needed. I severely underestimated the thousands of hours that I would dedicate to leadership and the negative impact on the rest of the team of a lack of leadership training. The importance of leadership to your culture cannot be overstated. Often we elevate good technicians from our team to leadership positions, but we often fail to provide specific leadership training.

I was in a call just yesterday when someone said to me, "I love how you are on time for our meetings." I questioned why they were bringing this up and was told that a prior leader showed up late to all of their meetings or would just "ghost" them. Whaaaaaaaat? Are you kidding? Who does that? Surely not a caring leader. I cannot even comprehend the thought of ghosting someone on our team, much less multiple times. Such a lack of respect. I did not fully appreciate how important it was for me to offer the most basic leadership training. Also, fundamental personal accountability was missing. It never occurred to me that I needed to confirm that someone was showing up on time for meetings. Trust and verify—my new accountability mantra. I have burned myself again and again by failing to verify that someone is doing what they say they are doing. Now that the verification process is built into their work process, I know when things are being accomplished. The saying "Hire slowly and fire fast" is such great advice. If someone is not meeting expectations in the first ninety days of employment, it is unlikely that this will improve over time. I have shifted my mindset from making excuses for others to accepting that people show you who they are through their actions. This goes back to the hiring process, however; if we are seeing any red flags in the hiring process, we must pass on that candidate. Historically, we noted the red flags but often made excuses for them or discussed how we would work around them. That does not happen currently. Core-value red flags during the hiring process are going to be full-blown fires shortly into their tenure.

Another challenge of our fast growth was that the operational structure was not sturdy enough to support the growth—that is, the systems were not tested and utilized sufficiently, and the decision-making process was not fast enough to adapt. This stalls everything and creates discontent. I have seen decisions just languish for months, but a small business needs speed. Having layers of untrained leaders can cause decision paralysis. Training was needed to help people understand how to move a decision forward—come to the table with three researched options, provide one recommendation and the analysis of why that is your recommendation, and explain the timing need for this particular decision and the impact of any delays. Again, this was an accountability issue all on me.

A soul-crushing challenge of fast growth was the core-value misalignment of several team members, which ultimately resulted in a diluted customer service experience. Hearing from an unhappy client that they did not feel cared for by their legal team was a stab in the heart to me. Care is vitally important to me—self-care, team care, and client care. When it became clear that we had some team members who did not value care, I realized that it was time to "burn it all down." Well, maybe not to that extreme, but I knew we had team members who needed to be exited misalignment. This "burning" process has been difficult, but it has also been the best thing for our culture and our clients. We are acutely aligned around our core values now, and that alignment is seen in happier clients, better client reviews, and better team collaboration.

Finally, a financial challenge of rapid growth is the creep of costs, both labor costs and operational expenses. There are so many moving parts that you stop looking at many of the smaller numbers, but those small numbers add up quick. You might overlook a 5-10 percent drop in productivity or a $250 expense here or there or another administrative hire. Ignore the little numbers at your peril. I re-read *Profit First* by Michael Michalowicz toward the end of 2022 and realized that I had overlooked the cost creep. I was looking at expenses and discovered charges that I had never heard of before. I didn't even know what they were. I also discovered that our administrative costs were quite high and not in line with industry norms. So after about 100 hours digging into every number, including the ROI on each and every team member, I made several expense adjustments in both labor and operational expenses in order to create a more fiscally responsible business. The Profit First method of looking at Revenue − Profit = Expenses is a game-changing way to view your finances and allows for consistent, incremental improvements to get your percentages where they need to be.

Mario Godoy

I started my law firm right out of law school. For those of you doing the same, it's likely your first challenge will be self-doubt. You will also face criticism from well-meaning people who are triggered by your plan.

Remember, this is your race. You don't need anyone's approval. Personally, I like to make certain decisions by asking myself, "Will I regret not doing this at the end of my life?"

You need to ask yourself who will really be worse off when you are successful. The list of people who will be better off when you are successful will be much longer.

There Is No Finish Line

It's a very different path for lawyers who work for another law firm, then decide to start their own practice. They've seen things they want to do differently, and they want run a law firm, a business, their own way, trying out their own ideas.

Learning to run a law firm, a business, without having ever worked in one may be the harder way, but for me it was motivational, and challenging—two things I thrive on. Being a self-starter and being willing to try new things and risk failure are traits I enjoy, even though this approach can be frustrating and lead to a lot of mistakes.

Owning any business will have its up and downs. More than a decade after starting my firm, I have challenges in my current business. I am still trying to get to the next level. There is no finish line in business unless you decide to stop. Fortitude is a key component to being successful as a small business owner.

You will need to resist the urge to judge yourself by someone else's progress. There are those ahead of you who started earlier than you. Some had more capital to start. It's important to keep your perspective along the way. Its important to measure your progress against your past self. Even a one percent improvement every week can add up over the course of time.

Don't Be Afraid to Ask for Help

I interned at the state's attorney's office and passed the bar exam in July, and in November I got my license. To learn how to get clients, manage cases, and build a legal practice, I cold-called attorneys and asked for advice on starting my own firm.

Everyone told me to get a job at a firm. But that wasn't what I wanted; I wanted to have my own law firm, not work for someone else. Along the way, I was fortunate to meet a few "legal guardian angels," Robert Smith and Mary L. Field.

Bob taught me how to be a lawyer. He gave me legal work and then would meet me for lunch and help me by providing templates and talking through whatever problems I was facing. Mary taught me how to practice immigration law—and in return, I offered to pay her part of my fee to review my work. After two or three years, I finally knew enough to earn a living. I keep in touch with Mary and Bob to this day.

Almost every year, I hire one or two young interns with almost zero experience to help them and get them started, the same way I was helped by my legal guardian angels. And I've hired three of them to work at Godoy Law Office after they became attorneys.

Don't be afraid to approach other attorneys to ask for mentorship or help. Think outside the box to discover what you can help them with. And always look for opportunities to pay it forward in our profession.

Don't Play the Victim

People often see success and assume that the person has always been successful at all times.

Part of transitioning to CEO is learning to control your emotions. I think that whenever you play to win, you put your heart on the line. As a CEO, you are going to be put in many different scenarios. You are not going to get everyone of those scenarios right. Part of growing into a CEO is having the humility to know that you will not always be right. It's okay to feel moments of doubt. It's *not* okay to act on feelings alone.

It's also not good to ignore your feelings. We are all human. Acknowledging your emotions is part of the journey.

When I am feeling especially emotional, I like to take a couple of hours or days to process the feelings. I like to self-reflect and ask myself, "What is life trying to teach me right now?" or "Why is this happening for me?" I surround myself with a board of advisers that act as an independent sounding board.

People think that champions don't get knocked down. The truth is they do get knocked down; they learn to embrace failure and learn from it. Over and over again. The champion is the person who picks themself up and keeps moving forward.

As you transition to CEO, remember that the circumstances may not be in your favor, but being unconquerable is a choice.

Michelle Dellino

When I started my firm in 2013, I expected my biggest challenge would be the one every person opening their doors thinks about—getting clients. How would I find them? How would they find me? Would it just be me on Facebook all day, hoping someone would call me? It took a couple of years, but that challenge and the fear associated with it faded as my firm (Dellino Family Law Group or "DFLG") became established. The clients never stopped coming. I was on to worrying about new things as I moved into the early iterations of the CEO role.

Once things got moving and clients were consistently coming in the door, the challenges of scaling a practice as the firm's leader began to present themselves. Nothing scared me—I dropped out of high school, was arrested in my youth, survived multiple bouts with cancer, and had to start over more times than I cared to count. I felt invincible, so I figured starting a law firm and charting my course to move into the CEO seat would be no sweat. I was wrong about that, but if you know more than I did going in and surround yourself with people you can trust, you will be able to anticipate the challenges and plan ahead for them.

The People

Let's start with the people. This may very well be your biggest challenge. In a services business and profession, the people are everything. They are the clients, the team, the production. You cannot succeed as a CEO and your firm cannot thrive without the right people in the right seats.

One of the people I trust most told me in my first year of my own firm that the people would be the hardest part. I had no idea what he was talking about, but time has proven him was right. It

64

was all easy for me at first. I was loving my work and building my firm, so adding people just seemed natural, and I expected they would just do what I would do. That, obviously, is not how it works. No one else will do things the way you do or have the exact same values or prior experience. Everyone you work with will bring their own history and approaches that you will have to understand and fold into your team.

Having the right people in the right seats can make or break your team. You will feel the challenge in the best ways when you have the right people and need to learn how to maximize their skills so they and the firm can thrive. You will feel the challenge in the worst way when you have the wrong people or not enough people. I think about approaching the "people" challenge in two different categories. First, the people you already have, including the interpersonal and workplace issues associated with having a team of different people. This is human nature—and exactly why you eventually need HR help, but more on that later. Second, the staffing issues you will have both growing and keeping your team.

You might be in a busy metropolitan area; in which case you will have the challenge of attracting and retaining quality staff. You might go through a cycle where there are plenty of attorneys, and you will need to make sure you do your due diligence to hire only the talent that comports with your core values. You might also be in a cycle where talent is scarce, and you will need to avoid what I call "desperation hires," where anyone will do to get the work done. This never ends well. In rough markets for hiring, you will have other firms seeking to poach your staff on a regular basis, whether it is on LinkedIn, via email, or at conferences and social events. Even people you thought were friends or supportive colleagues may do this. You will learn not to trust everyone. To keep the valuable team you have, you will need to let your core values shape your culture, be real with your team, and get to know them and what they need. Then you will need to deliver it. If people are good culture fits and know you have their backs, they won't want to leave when that colleague on the other side of town slides into their LinkedIn inbox asking if they want to have a conversation about a new role.

You will also have to evaluate your own values when it comes to dealing with the challenge of staffing. Will you also poach talent from other firms? Will you use recruiters and budget for that? Perhaps you will prefer to play the long game, developing relationships to nurture a pipeline of potential team members. There are so many different ways to approach staffing, and no one way or combination of approaches is right or wrong. My advice to you is to figure out what works with your values and needs, set up a system, and stick with it. You need your staffing system to include how you will find team members, what your hiring funnel will look like, and how you will evaluate who joins your team and who doesn't. You will also need a second, equally important system for evaluating the team you have on an ongoing basis while you develop and manage them.

It is going to be a lot of work. When it comes to the "people" issues, this part of the work never ends. I find that it has gotten easier as I have learned to avoid the bad hires, handle the internal issues that come up with the team, and stay true to my values and systems. But it is still always a challenge. The people can be the very best and most fun part of being the CEO—or the very worst. Do yourself a favor and lock in your "people systems" early on. You will make mistakes, but be sure to learn from them. When someone shows you who they are, believe them the first time, good or bad. Be with the people you want to be with, but keep the focus on putting together the best possible team for your clients.

The Growth

At DFLG, we experienced quick growth right out of the gate. Within a year we were grossing one million, and within three years we were over two million. Since then, as we are moving through year ten, we have consistently increased revenue and the size of the team. We added "growth" to our core values at the firm this year. I have realized that to be a good fit for our team and do well, you have to be comfortable challenging yourself to grow. You must also understand that the firm is always growing and changing—it is not a static environment. We are committed to growing not only as legal professionals, but also as people and as a business. This kind of growth can be rewarding but also turbulent. It can be exciting but also precarious. Acknowledging that growth is imperfect and will never look exactly how you expected is the best way to start. Once you acknowledge that, the more you can plan for your team's growth and lead it—especially after you cross the one million threshold—the smoother things will be for you and the team as a whole.

The Isolation

No one told me about this challenge, but I will tell you that being the CEO and leader of your firm can be isolating. It is lonely. When you are the boss, you cannot talk to your staff about all the internal issues, how you feel about them, the people, the challenges, and the ups and downs. You can be authentic and share some of this, and you should, but you cannot be friends and vent the way coworkers can with everyone else on the team over a happy hour. You are the leader and a boss, so much of that is inappropriate in that role. On top of that, no one else will fully understand the weight on your shoulders and the roller coaster of emotions that the CEO role can bring. You will hopefully form a leadership team at some point, and that will be a critical sounding board for you. You will have your go-to people for advice. But being CEO is different from being another team member or even being a manager. There is only one of you.

You can deal with the isolation by having your own communities. Connecting with the CEOs of other law firms is essential. You will learn from them, and they will learn from you. You can and should tell your spouse or close friends about the challenges you will face leading your team, but they won't feel it the same way another person in the same role will, and they won't have the same level of helpful feedback. You cannot do this all alone. Do not try to exist in a vacuum, and do not treat your team like friends when it comes to discussing challenges. Find your people and your support system.

Billie Tarascio

Every year of owning Modern Law has been different. In *Tiger Tactics I*, I talked about challenges with marketing, technology, vision, and people. In this book, I'm going to talk about the challenges I have experienced as the CEO of Modern Law from pre-pandemic to today. During this period, we grew from a firm creating $2m in revenue to $5m in revenue—or, to put it another way, from fifteen people to thirty-five people. The needs of the firm changed rapidly based on our size just as the needs of our employees and clients were changing because of the events taking place in our country. It's been a wild ride full of challenges.

When you move fast, you don't experience fewer challenges, you just experience them simultaneously or in quicker succession. My pre-pandemic law firm and post-pandemic law firm are two very different places to work in and to lead. Our pre-pandemic culture was undisciplined and unaccountable. It was a clan culture based on relationships between colleagues. That culture is simply not scalable. As we grew, we needed accountability. People had to follow the systems we put in place to protect the firm and the clients. My team was not that team. When the pandemic hit, we easily transitioned to a work-from-home organization. We had always had the capability of working from home, but we culturally preferred to work in the office. After six months of work from home, there was no going back. Relationships between people at work suffered. At the same time, demand for legal services was greater than ever. Our revenue soared. People became depressed and overworked. We needed to hire to keep up with demand.

It turned out that many people in my organization were not cut out to work in a larger firm. Some did not want the structure required to run a larger organization. Some were underperformers being exposed and outperformed by newer colleagues. Mostly, the firm lacked the infrastructure needed to support a larger team and more clients. We didn't have systems for management or enough managers. We didn't have enough people supporting human resources, billing, accounting, or technology within the firm. Our cultural traditions that had helped us thrive as a younger, smaller firm were disastrous at a larger firm. I needed to learn new skills. But I didn't know how, and I didn't even know what I was missing. The other challenge was that I had built my firm to be experimental. If something wasn't working, the thought was, change it and try something else. That worked when we were a small, clan culture, but it was hugely detrimental to my larger team.

My people were experiencing too much turmoil and stress outside of work worrying about their families, their health, and the economy to handle the chaotic and invigorating environment of an ever-changing startup that was no longer a startup. The turnover in 2021-2022 was astronomical. This caused more stress and chaos in my team and my clients. My employees were not well-behaved. We had factions and cliques. We had high performers who followed the rules and resented anyone who didn't. We had paralegals banding together and deciding they could refuse to do work an attorney asked them to do if it was outside our written procedures. We had plenty of people who hated the managers I had put in place and would only report to or work directly for me. It was a mess.

I had to slow down. I had to take a big step back. Our foundation was not built for the law firm we had become. Instead of patching holes and dealing with drama, we needed to reinforce and rebuild the foundation. We needed a structure to work within so that everyone would know what to expect. We went back to our values and our law firm constitution. Our values were written in long paragraph form within our law firm constitution. Like our US Constitution, it contained structural and procedural elements as well as aspirational values. Our constitution contained a great number of procedures and expectations but no accountability. Very few people followed our written procedures, and our constitution did not contain any consequences for failing to meet expectations or follow procedure.

If you firm is always growing, what your firm needs from you is always changing. There is truly no playbook. Each of my chapters will focus on the specific changes I have needed to make to get from $2m to $5m in terms of tools, people, and the vision for the future.

Jay Ruane

For me, there have been both internal and external challenges, and both have their ways of sneaking up on you.

On the internal side, I think all of us are plagued with some degree of impostor syndrome. As you learn more, you also learn how much more you don't know. And that can be frightening. Many of us, while quite confident in our legal skills after three years of head-to head competition with our classmates for ranking (which didn't end up mattering at all to about 90 percent of us) feel inadequate when we consider our place in the business world. I get it—it's a big deal to make payroll every week committing to others who rely on you for their actual survival.

But impostor syndrome is only one of the internal challenges you will face. Another will be lack of time. For me, I feel like I am always running full speed. Like sprinting. I always know there are a dozen more things I want to do, and these don't even include the things I *have* to do. I need to be able to admit that I will not get everything done, and I need to be be OK with that. The personal perception of lack of time can make you neglect the other parts of you—your health, your family, your life outside your business. While going "all in" is seen by many as total commitment, that type of commitment 24/7/365 is unhealthy, and for many of us, it negatively impacts our social, mental, and physical health. I wish I had the answers to this problem for you, but it is one you must address on your own at the right time. All platitudes from outsiders can do is give you guilt. They can't make you change your course.

Time management is a critical skill for any lawyer entrepreneur because simple decisions can dramatically escalate into big problems if you do not make decisions timely. You can lose first-mover advantage in a new vertical to someone else (which happened to me, although I survived and thrived) You can fail to act timely with marketing, costing you hundreds or tens of thousands of dollars by being late to the game or choosing the wrong vehicle to get you someplace. You can get stuck in the minutiae, paralyzed with the fear you will make the wrong choice, and thereby make none, further sabotaging yourself. But throughout the process, you will need to embrace your newfound role and make sure you are truly getting all you can out of it.

The two major problems see with scaling law firms is that they are undercapitalized or understaffed. Usually the second happens because of the first, but both can hurt the firm deeply.

Understaffing is common in law firms. How many of us would go to a restaurant where the same person greeted us, seated us, served us drinks, cooked and served the food, cleaned up afterward, and took our payment? You would think that restaurateur was crazy, and you would be right.

But how many law firms have one person filling the role of host, maître d',, waitstaff, chef, bartender, and busboy? Have you considered that? Nothing can be great if people aren't able to focus on what they excel at. There is a reason professional sports teams have a bunch of players (some with certain specialties) they can tap when needed. The wonderful thing about the practice of law in 2023 is that borders are somewhat irrelevant and remote assistance can solve a lot of staffing —with the correct training, of course. Staffing is expensive; I know this personally. But understaffing? That can be far more ruinous long-term.

The biggest challenge almost everyone who launches a firm will face is undercapitalization. We simply don't launch with the reserves to match what we need to survive until profitable. And I get that many who launch do so because the rug was pulled out from under them. Others launch for pride or ego but have never really built a business plan other than "I can do this." Every dollar you spend early in your firm's existence is a dollar you cannot spend elsewhere.

Even today, with millions in revenue, I sometimes flinch at the smallest expense, while smiling when I walk into much greater ones. There seems to be no rhyme or reason, but I am who I am. What I have decided to do is simple. I figured out what I needed to 1. Live with a certain level of comfort and 2. Reinvest the rest into the firm. In the past, my firm bought me a car, and when that was paid off, I realized I didn't need a new one, so I still drive my nine-year-old car. Making smart choices with money allows me the flexibility to take fliers on other ideas I may have, but I try to run this firm in a way that never prevents me from spending when money needs to be spent. I am willing to forgo profit because even after twenty years of running this firm, I still view myself as a small firm just trying to scale more—even if I'm not sure whether that is what I really want to do. More on that later in this book.

Jenn Gore-Cuthbert

There will be many challenges along the way, and it's important to maintain a positive attitude and a willingness to persevere. I have always believed that failure is not an option and that giving up is never an acceptable solution. However, there have been many instances when my mindset was tested to its limits. I can vividly recall moments over the years when staff members handed in their resignations, leaving me with a deep sense of uncertainty and anxiety.

No matter what the situation—key people quitting, terminating underperforming or non—culture-fit employees, hiring the wrong person, facing cash flow challenges, making continual mistakes and wasting resources, or dealing with unhappy (and sometimes unreasonable) clients—every challenge has presented an opportunity for growth and learning. Instead of dwelling on setbacks, remember to continually ask, "What is the lesson in this mistake?" By thinking this way, you can transform challenges into opportunities and emerge stronger and more resilient.

Losing Key People

Dealing with the departure of a "key person" from your team can be tough. It's not just the loss of their skills and experience, but also the impact on team morale and client relationships. It's important to take steps to address the situation and move forward:

- First, don't panic! Although it may feel like a big setback, try to remain calm and avoid making hasty decisions.
- Assess the situation and the impact of the employee's departure on your law firm.
- Develop a transition plan to ensure work continues smoothly. Consider identifying a replacement or distributing responsibilities among other employees.

- Be transparent with your team about the situation and your plan for moving forward. This can help maintain a positive work environment and alleviate anxiety.
- If possible, conduct an exit interview with the departing employee to gather feedback and identify areas for improvement.
- Use the experience as an opportunity to evaluate your hiring and retention practices. Implement changes to prevent similar situations in the future.

Making the Wrong Hire

Making the wrong hire is tough, but it happens to every one of us. It can be challenging to invest time and resources in a new employee only to realize that they aren't meeting your expectations. When this happens, it's essential to act quickly to minimize the negative impact on your firm and your team.

Schedule a meeting with the employee to discuss their performance, and provide specific feedback. Together, create a performance improvement plan that outlines goals and deadlines. Be sure to monitor progress and provide regular feedback to help the employee improve. In some cases, termination may be necessary, so follow your company's policies and procedures. Afterward, take the opportunity to reflect on what you learned, and consider making changes to prevent similar issues in the future. Again, remember that every challenge presents an opportunity for growth and improvement.

Managing Contingency Cash Flow

Running a contingency business can be quite challenging when it comes to managing cash flow. Unfortunately, there are typically a variety of external factors that could impact your income in a contingency law business. Some of the challenges that you might face include uncertainty regarding case resolution timing and value, which can lead to unpredictability in your cash flow. This can make it difficult to plan for future expenses and create financial stability for the law firm.

Fortunately, there are several steps you can take to handle cash flow problems. You should create a budget that outlines your expected expenses and revenue. You should also create a cash forecast model based on predictive case resolutions. This can help you forecast cash flow and identify potential cash flow problems before they occur. I highly recommend checking out the book *Fireproof* by Michael Morse and John Nachazel for some great tips and advice on budgeting, cash forecasting, and profitability.

Another option is to improve your cash flow management by focusing on increasing efficiencies in case inventory management. You should be looking for ways to streamline workflows and move cash quicker, for example, "fast-tracking" cases that already are worth the policy limits. On the other end, cash flow problems can improve if you push to increase your case values. You should increase the percentage of cases in litigation to push for cases that resolve for their maximum value. Finally, you can also explore financing options such as lines of credit or loans to even out cash flow and provide immediate access to cash when you need it. However, you should always seek loans or lines of credit well before you need them.

Managing Unhappy Clients

Dealing with an unhappy client can be a real challenge for any law firm. That's why it's important to take steps to avoid these situations in the first place. Here are a few things that law firms can do to keep their clients happy and satisfied:

Clear communication is key. It's important for law firms to clearly explain the services they'll provide, the timelines involved, and the fees associated with their services. This can help to avoid any confusion or misunderstandings down the road.

Managing client expectations is also crucial. Lawyers should be honest with clients about what they can and can't do for them, as well as what the potential outcomes of their legal matter might be. This can help to avoid any unrealistic expectations and ensure that clients are satisfied with the results.

Setting realistic deadlines and providing regular updates to clients is also important. Lawyers should be proactive in communicating any delays or issues that may arise and should provide updates on the progress of the case on a regular basis. This can help to avoid any surprises and keep clients informed about the status of their case.

Of course, providing quality service is also essential. Lawyers should be responsive to client needs, answer questions promptly, and keep clients informed about the status of their case. Building trust and loyalty with clients can lead to positive reviews and referrals, which are always a good thing.

Owner's Mindset as the Greatest Challenge

As a business owner, it's important to recognize that your mindset can have the biggest impact on the success of your business. Your personality, beliefs, values, experiences, and emotions can all shape your perspective, decision-making, and overall approach to running the business.

If you have a negative or fixed mindset, you may be resistant to change and dismissive of new ideas. This can limit your business's potential for innovation and growth. On the other hand, if you have a growth mindset and an optimistic outlook, you may be more open to new opportunities and willing to take calculated risks. This can help your business thrive and reach its full potential.

Your mindset can also impact how you interact with your employees, clients, colleagues, and mentors. If you have a micromanaging or controlling mindset, you may struggle to trust and empower your team. This can lead to a lack of motivation and productivity. But if you have a collaborative leadership mindset, you can foster a culture of teamwork, communication, and shared vision. One thing is for sure: the owner's mindset is an area that perpetually needs improvement and reflection to continue growing. Remember: new level, new devil.

Ryan McKeen

If you decide that this journey from lawyer or someone running a small law firm to CEO is for you, then this may be the most important chapter in this book. The challenges you are signing up for are unlike the challenges that you have faced before. Knowing what lies ahead is the key to pushing through it all.

When I started out as a solo, I had to do everything. I did books, reception, intake, marketing, trials, and janitorial services for my firm. I had to learn a lot. Prior to opening my own firm, I had never opened QuickBooks. Suddenly, I had to learn QuickBooks while trying to do all the other things that needed doing. It wasn't terribly fun, nor was it all that productive.

When I wrote the original *Tiger Tactics*, I took what I had learned doing those things and wrote them down. Documenting what you do and how you do it is the act of building systems. Then the challenge becomes hiring people to run those systems. This works for a while, and if you do it right, it will change your practice and your life. However, this is not part of the challenge of being a CEO. If becoming a law firm CEO was an Everest expedition, at this point you are at basecamp.

If you keep building systems, improving your marketing, and hiring people, then your organization will become more and more complicated.

I always think about this when making restaurant reservations. There was a time when our entire team could sit at a high top in a bar. Then we needed a booth. And then we needed to reserve a large table. The challenge comes when you can no longer all fit at a large table. Suddenly, even getting a restaurant reservation is a challenge. You may have to call weeks in advance and reserve a room, or it may be entirely impossible, depending on where you live.

Also, lunch is going to cost a lot more. What used to be a $50 bill for two to three people suddenly becomes a $1000 tab. What used to be simple is suddenly way more complicated and time-consuming. You can no longer just walk into a restaurant and be seated. No restaurant does that when you have a party of thirty.

It is at this point, you begin to understand the challenges of being a CEO. This restaurant analogy will play itself out over and over again in your practice. Case review sessions that once took an hour will end up taking a day, then several days, and then a week, and then they become impossible.

The one-on-one meetings that you did on Friday afternoons to build your team will become impossible unless you wish to have a week of nothing but one-on-one meetings with your team.

All of this is made more difficult if you, like me, have bootstrapped your entire practice financially. In that case, it is unlikely you will have the money to hire the people you need when you first need them to do things like make restaurant reservations or do one-on-ones for you. And as an added bonus, your team will grow large enough that the demands on you will increase at the same moment that you are probably facing increasing demands from clients on legal work.

Many small law firms operate like close-knit families in the best sense of the term. People know about each other's kids and lives. But if you are going to transition to becoming a CEO, that will have to change. You can have those kind of relationships with five people, but things start to strain somewhere around twenty. At that point, you may know things about the people who are on your team, but the depth of the relationships isn't there. And then things change even more until you don't know those things, and maybe one day you won't even know the names of everyone on your team (I'm not there yet).

And this right here is the real challenge you will face. You will face it over and over every single day as you grow.

On the financial side, you will also face challenges. I think these boil down to two kinds. The first is that growth eats cash. In order to grow, you will need to spend more money on marketing and on payroll. Where are you going to get the cash that you will need? How are you going to manage your cash flow? This is an area you will spend a lot of time thinking about.

There was also a mindset component to me. In order to become CEO of my law firm, I had to get comfortable with very large numbers. My weekly payroll is now what I used to earn in six months as a solo or small firm owner. Whether it is through talking with your accountant or your therapist, you must get comfortable with expenses that are many multiples of what you are likely paying now.

Growing up middle class, never making money as a lawyer, and having no savings to speak of, getting comfortable with big numbers was harder for me than the practical side of generating the revenues necessary or managing cash flow.

This leads me to the biggest challenge of all. And that challenge is you. You will be the biggest barrier to both your success and the success of your firm. The number of peers that you have will shrink. The number of books or conferences that can move the needle will shrink. The low-hanging fruit both in your firm and your life will be picked.

Your challenge is to level up. The challenge of challenges is learning, adapting, and getting comfortable with facing your firm's biggest challenges and leading your team through them. You will have to do work on yourself.

Bill Umansky

Let's be honest, this will be a difficult journey. You must have the desire to run your practice because YOU want to be the boss. You cannot be too prepared to deal with the challenges. If you opened your own practice solely based on your ego, because you have a crappy boss, you hate authority or you simply just want to make more money, listen carefully. In order to deal with the barrage of challenges you must face as the leader of a growing law firm, you must have a passion for creating something in your image or external vision. Establish your purpose to create a business for you, your family, and your employees.

I could give you over a hundred challenges you will face, but in my opinion, you would get too stressed out reading about them and get lost in the weeds. I want to focus your attention on the largest challenges I have continued to face, predictably, in my more than thirty years of practice.

The first and largest challenge you will face running or growing a law firm is people! Sounds obvious, doesn't it? Well, a lot of younger lawyers believe that with artificial intelligence replacing humans, hard-working international virtual assistants, as well as intake, client relationship management (CRM) software, and other software, issues related to humans are something of the past. There are some areas of law where the foregoing can be applied to cut down on human drama. For example, certain translational areas that are form-driven can be done by artificial intelligence and virtual assistants using great software to provide legal products for the end consumer.

but what about most of us who litigate in court or deal with negotiating and drafting contracts with business owners, defending someone who has been arrested, or prosecuting insurance companies and negligent parties for the injured? Who deals with opposing counsel, the judges, and most of all, the clients who need to communicate their desires and their hurt, anger, grief, and anxiety? Lawyers, of course, and their cadre of paralegals and support staff that make up the team. When you grow larger, who manages the team? A robot? Of course not! Don't tell me you can third-party all your HR out-of-house at a litigation firm if you are trying to build a solid team. Who runs the finances, the hires and fires, and overseas operations? Managers, of course. And since we are all humans with varying degrees of ego and personal problems, baggage will be brought to work.

Specifically, I have found that your teammates can be the largest stressor of running a business. How many times in your short career have you caught yourself saying, "Why can't I just have employers that get along? Why do they bring their personal drama into the office? Why does A continue down a path of self-destruction when we give them all the tools they need? Why is it that I do everything for them, care for them, and it is still not enough?" And before you blame it on poor leadership, lack of values, bad training, or bad hiring, I can tell you that even with solid leadership, great hiring, training, and consistent core values, you will still have people problems. Why? Because we are human. We are flawed, and even if we are satisfied for the moment, most humans are not living authentic lives, chasing their dreams, or even holding themselves accountable for their happiness. And because lawsuits against employers have risen, we cannot even take personal chances to really dive down deep on a personal level with our team members to coach them on how to be a true professional, as most problems with employees unfortunately stem from personal issues such as lack of self-esteem, overblown egos, and a lack of introspection.

To complicate things further, younger employees want to work less and do not plan on sticking around for long. Regardless of what you give them, they are influenced by pop culture, their own friends, and the incessant noise that unless you open your own shop, you must be failing. In that environment, how could young law firm owners help but find people are the number-one challenge?

Joey Vitale

There's no shortage of challenges you will face as a law firm owner. In my experience, the following three challenges have been the most difficult to overcome. But at the same time, when I look back, I have also experienced the most personal and business growth by confronting these three challenges.

As one of my coaches says, "The biggest reason why your business isn't more successful is because you aren't yet willing to handle the problems associated with that next level of success." So if you're struggling to reach that next level of success in your firm, the path is likely through these three challenges—not around them.

Challenge #1: Judgment

Growing a law firm is actually pretty simple, at least in theory: if you want to get more leads and clients, just get more visible and make more offers.

But if you're like most law firm owners I know, then drawing more attention to yourself and your firm will be one of the scariest things you'll ever do. Getting visible can be extremely uncomfortable—posting videos, networking, asking for reviews, pitching yourself to potential referral partners, speaking on a podcast or a stage, and the list goes on.

It's inevitable that you'll face a ton of rejection. People will tell you no. A lot. If you're like most of us, this will test the limits of your comfort zone.

Finish this sentence: "If I get louder about my law firm, I'm afraid that ..."

How did you complete the statement? Afraid that prospects might think you're salesly? That family might think you're greedy? That your kids might think you're embarrassing? That other attorneys might think you're stupid for saying something wrong?

Or, even worse, that if no one engages with your content, it means you're worthless and don't matter?

Well, let me save you about $20,000 worth of coaching with this golden nugget of wisdom. What you're actually afraid of isn't what others will say or think about you. What you're afraid of is that what others say or think about you is true. Read that again.

So let's just cut to the core here. Do YOU think you're salesly? Greedy? Boring? Stupid? Not worthy? If the answer is no, then all you have to do is remember that. And then feel your fear of judgment fade away.

The louder you get, the faster your firm will grow. Staying the world's best-kept secret isn't doing your firm any favors. Any judgment you face doesn't mean a thing if you know that what they're saying isn't true. Stay confident and start taking up more space.

Challenge #2: Stress

Here's a not-so-fun fact: over 70 percent of entrepreneurs have self-reported mental health concerns. And the statistics are even worse for us lawyers. I don't know about you, but I've battled with stress a lot. As I shared in Chapter 1, I suffered horrible panic attacks during my first year as a law firm owner.

How are we supposed to handle all this stress? Well, I can share from experience what's worked well for me.

First off, I want to emphasize the power of therapy and take away any shame or embarrassment you may have about the idea of going to a therapist. I continue to speak with my therapist every month, and I know many other successful firm owners who do the same.

Second, consider joining a mastermind or coaching program. Having a person or group that I can count on to support me, where I can get raw and real, has been an absolute game changer. There are plenty of options out there. Reach out to me or any author in this book, and we'll be happy to give you our best recommendations based on your situation and needs.

Third, make an intentional effort to shift your focus to the present moment. This may come in the form of meditation, prayer, a gratitude exercise, or even just active listening. The more you are able to refocus your attention on the present moment, the less stressed you'll become. They say that depression is worrying about the past, while anxiety is worrying about the future. You prevent both when you tap into the here and now.

Fourth, don't sweat the small stuff, and realize that just about everything is small stuff. You've gotten through everything life has thrown at you so far; you can get through this, too. One thing I love to do is to treat all my business issues like a video game (I grew up playing a lot of Zelda on the N64). The thing about video games is that there is always a solution designed into every level—you just have to look hard or get creative to find it. Learn to love the game of business.

I've come to understand that if I'm going to reach that next level of success, then I need to keep leaning in and playing—and enjoying—the game in front of me, instead of wishing I could fast forward through the hard times to get to the good part. The journey is the destination. This is the good part.

Challenge #3: Ego

Now, if you're like most lawyers, you're pretty competitive. Heck, I'm your classic middle-child peacemaker, and I have to admit that I'm competitive, too. That's not a bad thing. But there are consequences to our default personalities that we need to be aware of.

As lawyers, we are a stubborn bunch. We don't like to lose. We're perfectionists. And while our egos may help us be great lawyers, they can also make us highly ineffective business owners and leaders.

What's a great way to overcome your ego? Take on the identity of a scientist instead of a perfectionist. A perfectionist always asks, "Why is this happening to me?" A scientist, on the other hand, will ask, "What can I learn from this?" By replacing perfectionism with curiosity, you'll be able to own your ego instead of letting your ego own you.

Managing our egos can be especially difficult because our egos drove us to become not only lawyers but entrepreneurs as well. Your hard work, hustle, and quick-start tendencies may have helped you get this far. But strengths can also be weaknesses. If you want to scale, then it may be time to part ways with your inner entrepreneur. To choose trust over control. Inspiration over perfection. We over me. Leadership over entrepreneurship.

Allison Williams

I remember the first time a business coach told me I could not continue to handle sixty-plus cases in fifteen counties across New Jersey if I wanted to build my law firm without it killing me in the process. A range of thoughts arose ... *He's not a lawyer; what does he know? I can do anything I set my mind to. So what if I almost died falling asleep driving when I was working ninety hours a week? I just haven't figured out the right mix of caffeine, energy drinks, catnaps, etc.*

So, I was definitely a workaholic—and NOWHERE near my 12-step program for it. But eventually, I asked myself why it was so challenging for me to think of leaving the court room. True, I loved every moment of it, but this was not about practicing law. This was about self-worth.

Who Am I without Lawyering?

So much of my identity had been wrapped up in being a successful lawyer. A powerful lawyer. A well-respected lawyer. Who would I be without lawyering?

If I left behind the courtroom and spent my time instead reviewing spreadsheets, monitoring KPIs, and training and developing my team, would I be as significant? Would I matter to my clients?

These questions ran through my mind and often hid behind more "logical" questions, such as:

Won't I be increasing my risk if other lawyers handle my client matters and then chose to leave the firm?

What if I hire a lawyer who screws something up and I get sued? Or worse, I get smacked with a grievance? (Punchline: both things have happened.)

How can I train a lawyer to be as good as me unless I allow them to see my lawyering firsthand?

In my mind, I simply could not be effective at training up lawyers and creating an ethically sound, success-driven company without doing it the way lawyers have been doing it since the beginning of the profession. I was stuck in my mind and in my own "stinking thinking."

The New Freedom in Handcuffs

Eventually, with the help of several business coaches, I did get out of my own way. I finally stepped into a bigger version of myself and focused on creating the results I desired for my clients, not on my personal attachment to being the star in the story. And with that decision came freedom.

About three years from starting, I was no longer necessary to my business. I became the visionary. I decided what needed to happen, shared my strategic vision, and then watched the team go into action. I had more time on my hands than I'd had since elementary school! And, truth be told … I began to feel empty.

I was so unfulfilled that I began to use my time on social media to to offer guidance and support to other law firm owners who were trying to get to my new nirvana of limited work hours and a fully systematized business. From this downtime was born my coaching business, Law Firm Mentor, LLC.

Outgrowing Your "Hunger"

As a CEO, you will have three primary jobs: creating and sharing a vision, assembling a team, and allocating resources. Creating a vision is not challenging when you first get started. You envision more money, and you chase it. Pretty simple. But once you create a fully systematized business, vision can become challenging. If you remember the stress of building from scratch, the comfort of having significantly more income and time can lead you to become melancholy and to question the need to create more.

Continuing to create when your needs are already met is a different animal from hustling when you are hungry. You must direct the creative energy that built your law firm into something meaningful to you, or you will find yourself struggling. If you created a business, you are a creator. Creators needs to create. There are other challenges to having large swaths of free time— namely, how others will perceive that time.

Law Firm Mutiny

Often, once the owner of law firm achieves significant financial and time freedom, they will spend extended time out of the office. In their absence, work is being done, but if the owner is not sharing the value of his/her time away from the office with the employees, the owner may experience the all-too-common law firm mutiny. A mutiny occurs when members of the firm begin to feel that they are entitled to live the entrepreneurial life of "more time and more money" and begin to resent the owner for having achieved that lifestyle. They think, "I am here busting my ass every day while the owner is off eating bonbons." What these employees will rarely recall is your many sleepless nights, how you funded cash deficits with your personal credit card, or how many nights, weekends, and holidays you slaved away over a hot computer, chasing checks to make payroll.

Because you made it seem easy, the entitled employee(s) will believe that they have been treated unfairly as you are reaping the rewards of their labor. The disgruntled employee stews in the juices of their resentment until they attempt to pick up files in the heat of the night and scurry off to another firm, taking money, resources, work product, and several other employees with him/her to start anew elsewhere.

Many law firm owners interpret the mutiny to be "just desserts" or cosmic payback to them for having the audacity to make money. Alternatively, they recognize that it was the selection of employees and the communications (or lack thereof) that culminated in this event.

Thankfully, I have never personally experienced a mutiny. As one was planned, my loyal employees let me know, and I shut it down. Unfortunately, many others were not so lucky. This is why it is incredibly important to surround yourself with high-quality people, to extract low-vibrational people immediately, and to communicate intentionally around roles in the firm. You are entitled to your success—and the freedoms that come with it.

CHAPTER 3

The People You Will Need

Mario Godoy

A law firm's hiring plan ties to the business plan. Our big goal at Godoy Law is to help 1,000,000 make America their home. As the CEO, you need to know your long-term plan.

In my case, I intend to pass Godoy Law Office on, so I'm building the foundation for a time when I'm no longer with the firm. I choose to do what I can to train future leaders, but I also need to ensure the firm thrives in the interim so it can be passed on.

Remember, owners need to stretch their thinking decades into the future. Then they work backward to set mile markers to reach that future.

The questions become:

Where is this firm going in the next 10-20 years?

What does the firm need to look like in five years to reach this goal?

What mile markers do we need to reach along the way?

Who do we need on the team?

There is the organizational chart of today, and an organizational chart of five years from now—who does the firm need to get there?

"ABR"

Building blocks allow recruiting to become strategic—what talent do I have, and who do I need to recruit to get on this bus to meet our future needs?

I believe what Jim Collins says in *Good to Great*—get the right people on the bus and the right people in the right seats. And we have to manage out the wrong people on the bus.

Mario-ism:

Always be recruiting.

One or two times yearly, I chart and grade my staff using a system my dad taught me:

Are they good in their role at Godoy or not, and do they fit with our culture, our mission, our vision?

I categorize every team member:

- A Players: The unicorns. Keep them happy and working here. They are a good culture fit and are proficient.
- B Squad: Great culture fit, but not as technically proficient as an A player.
- D and F: They have to go. You know right away they don't fit, and they can't do the job.
- C are the tough ones: They can do the job, but they're not a good culture fit.

The C team is really a tough call for me because they get good results and can do the job. But in reality, you need to let them go. The C players can hurt the B players; the B players often look up to C players because they are technically proficient.

Who can be recruiting all the time? At Godoy, it's a challenge, and we have constant job posts and have a mantra of Always Be Recruiting. We reach out to our network and staff to find the passive job candidates. As an owner, you need to look at every interaction as an opportunity to find and recruit players.

As part of my annual chart exercise, for each team member, I also ask:

Given the opportunity, would I rehire them?

Future Needs

Networking, meeting people, and recruiting are planning for future needs—they're not always about the firm's needs today.

Recently I was interviewing a person I worked with in 2013. We've been touching base for ten years, and now there may be an opportunity to bring them on in a leadership role. Ten years ago, there was not a fit for either of us. But today, planning for where Godoy needs to be in two to five years, that person may be what we need.

You have to know where you're going and what talent you need for the future. People hop off your bus and get on someone else's bus unexpectedly. If you're always recruiting, you can have a bench of people ready to step in when someone leaves, your firm changes, or circumstances change.

One lesson it took me years to learn was to cross-train individuals on the team. You should ideally have someone on your team that can act as a Band-Aid until you hire the right person back into the system.

Where's the Welcome Wagon?

Onboarding is actually so much more important than recruiting. Businesses put so much focus on recruiting; then the people show up, and where's the welcome wagon? We've invested so much in recruiting, but what happens when the new hire shows up for work and you're not prepared?

Being ghosted by a new employee is expensive; don't give new hires buyer's remorse.

The first ninety days, new hires are trying to decide whether they want to work here. They are wondering if they want to build their future here. Are they here for more than a paycheck?

Making sure everyone has the same foundation and has the same goals is essential to having the same values. Over time, we've put an onboarding system in place. You can get a free copy of our list by going to https://godoylawoffice.com/onboarding.

Our new hires then get substantial training, classes, resources, and whatever they need to be successful on the job. Onboarding is ongoing: it doesn't end after X many days. People need constant development and reinforcement to grow and excel in their work for us and in their careers.

Never having worked in someone else's firm, part of my job as a CEO is to work on vertical alignment—aligning what I consider the firm's win with what the individual staff member considers a personal, professional, or financial win.

Vertical alignment means that everyone in the firm is aware of our law firm's goals, understands them, and is aware of how they as an individual contribute to the business's goals. It creates a win/win relationship. When the firm wins, we all win.

Understanding Individual Goals

Hiring and building the right team is one of the biggest challenges I faced—and still face—as the CEO of a law firm. When I hire staff attorneys, their goals are not necessarily the same as mine, the firm's, or the clients'.

Hiring people is a two-way scenario. People want to do well. They want to feel like they're contributing, like they're winning. Some people are motivated by money, others by time with family, others by recognition, and others by their vision and successes.

Figuring out what motivates each individual is key—we're not all on the same ship, we're all in the same body of water, and everyone is captain of their own ship. But a rising tide lifts all ships.

For law firms, that means everyone on the team has their own personal goals they want to achieve by working here. While everyone needs to work together to help our clients achieve their goals, each individual is responsible for their own happiness and satisfaction. And ultimately, if the law firm does well and is successful, we all do well. But that doesn't mean every team member will be happy and want to stay with the firm, and that every team member should stay. That's a hard lesson to learn.

Mario-ism:

We're not all on the same ship, but we're all in the same body of water and everyone is captain of their own ship.

I want every person we hire to know, one year into their tenure here, that choosing to work at Godoy was a good decision—personally, professionally ,and financially.

The Godoy Experience

You have to show your people that you give a sh*t about them. Our team members could have gone to work anywhere. We didn't just choose them; they chose Godoy. I want to sell the experience of working at Godoy. We ask recent hires, "Why did you take this job of all the jobs you could have taken?"

We want to find out about our team's families, what ice cream they like, and how they want to be rewarded—including the non-monetary rewards that matter to so much for job satisfaction but are unique to each individual.

You have to understand your people's "why."

Mario-ism:

You cannot overcommunicate as a manager.

Elise Buie

The People You Will Need—Unicorn Astronauts—Culture Is Everything

- Define your culture with your core values
- Use your core values as the filter for all decisions
- Talk about your core values regularly
- Celebrate based on your core values
- Use core values in the hiring process
- Use core values to exit misaligned team members
- Find out what motivates your team
- Care (actually give a f@@@ and show it) about your team
- Have the tough conversations
- Offer coaching and development opportunities
- Direct, compassionate feedback is a gift
- Psychological safety vs. challenging people to stretch

People are everything. You read that everywhere, hear it from all leaders, and it is 1000 percent true. But people are really only as good as your systems. If your hiring system is not foolproof, people will sneak into your firm who are misaligned with your culture. Or if your onboarding does not properly train new employees, even a great person can develop bad habits from day one that cause future problems. If you don't have systems for success and KPIs for every position, you can have an underperformer who flies under the radar for far too long, wreaking havoc on your culture. Don't invite a cancer into your firm due to poor systems. Systems, systems, systems are the key to people success..

Are you a helicopter parent? A micromanager? Or are you a "Google it" parent? You know exactly what I mean if you are a parent... Are you that parent who is sitting with your senior in high school as they do their college applications or are you the parent who has no idea where your child is applying for college? Be honest here, as this will likely determine your CEO leadership style as well. I was that mom who taught my kids to be quite independent early on—they cooked, cleaned, shopped for their clothes, and did their own laundry (starting in elementary school). They all had jobs starting in middle school, and we never paid anyone for chores or grades; chores were part of living with others and being on a family team, and grades determine your choices.

Based on my parenting style, it is not surprising that I am the type of leader who wants to teach someone how to find the answer and empower them to solve their own future problems. Maximizing others brings me joy. Micromanaging others is soul-crushing to me. *The New One Minute Manager* by Ken Blanchard was a great read on this topic. Some of my go-to questions when a team member is trying to put their monkey on my back: *How do you suggest you solve this problem? What solutions would be in the best interest of the firm? What information do you need to solve this problem? How can I support you in solving this problem?* These questions keep the responsibility in the hands of the team member while empowering them to seek solutions.

One way to test whether you are sufficiently empowering your team to make decisions without you is to be absent from your firm for multiple weeks. Each time I take this prolonged absence, we learn of new bottlenecks involving me. This information allows us to create better systems, including empowering everyone to make decisions. That could be scary if you do not have a fundamental basis for all decision-making. If all systems fail or if there is no system in place, empowering your team to make decisions on the fly is critical to your firm's well-being and your well-being. My team knows that any decision made from a place of excellence, integrity, and compassion is aligned with our core values. We cannot go too wrong if those three values underlie every decision.

Jenn Gore-Cuthbert

As the owner of the law firm, you will likely be the visionary, responsible for setting the direction of the firm and charting its course. However, to ensure that your vision becomes a reality, you will also need an integrator or second-in-command, who can help you manage the day-to-day operations of the firm and ensure that your ideas are executed successfully.

This integrator doesn't necessarily have to be another lawyer. When I first hired my law firm administrator, we worked well together. I would come up with ideas, and she would help me execute them. However, as our workload increased, we found ourselves stretched too thin and unable to manage everything effectively.

At this stage, many law firms get stuck, believing that hiring an integrator or COO is the only solution. However, to keep expanding and growing your firm, you will eventually need to develop an entire leadership team. This team will consist of the head of marketing, head of intake, head of legal, head of finance, head of HR, and head of IT/technology.

Developing leaders within your law firm is crucial to its long-term success. You don't want to create a "cast of assistants" who simply follow orders without any initiative or ownership. Instead, you want to cultivate a team of leaders who can step up and take ownership of their department's success. These leaders should have a "firm first" mentality and a genuine belief in the law firm's future.

However, it's important to be cautious when elevating people into leadership positions. Prematurely promoting someone to a leadership role can be dangerous for the firm and send the wrong message to your staff. It's essential to wait until a person has proven that they have the character and skills of a leader before giving them the responsibility of managing others. While there will undoubtedly be people who squander opportunities, there will also be those who seize them and excel.

Head of Marketing

The head of marketing manages your entire marketing strategy and budget, ensuring that it aligns with your law firm's goals. As the owner, you can still be involved in the marketing aspects of the firm, but the marketing director should take charge of analyzing all marketing data and making necessary adjustments. This includes meeting with vendors, providing internal reporting, and holding them accountable. A solid marketing plan with clear goals should be established every year during the last quarter of the prior year to guide the marketing strategy.

Head of Intake

The intake head coaches and manages the intake team regularly, audits decisions for quality control, assigns cases to legal teams, and reviews complex questions. They communicate with the marketing department about lead quality and effectiveness of marketing channels.

Head of Legal

For a law firm with multiple lawyers, the head of legal oversees legal teams led by associate attorneys. They ensure team goals are met and quality legal work is completed. This person coaches and mentors lawyers, answers complex legal questions, and audits cases for strategy and attorney skill set. As the owner, I previously held this role but found it time-consuming as the firm grew.

Head of Finance

The head of finance is critical for a growing law firm. They manage finances, handle payroll, and reconcile accounts. Our firm has a fractional CFO, bookkeeper, and CPA to ensure checks and balances. Regular financial reports are necessary to track progress and stay on budget.

Head of HR

As the firm grows, HR responsibilities become overwhelming. An HR professional can manage recruiting, benefits, employee pay, and compliance. A seasoned HR professional can make a huge difference, especially in recruiting top talent, which many law firms struggle with. Having a person dedicated to keeping the law firm staffed and growing is critical and gives you incredible leverage as the owner.

Head of IT/Technology

Tech management in a law firm requires an in-house IT person to manage all the technology, software, and equipment. A dedicated IT professional will be more available and think outside the box for your firm. Developing an IT plan and strategy for upgrading and maintaining all software and equipment is important for the long term.

You will need so many people to grow an incredible law firm, not just leaders but incredible people who work to support the legal team, such as a bubbly and bright receptionist and support for your leaders. I once heard the quote, "Whoever collects the most talent, wins"—talent war.

Domestic Support

This chapter would be incomplete if I didn't mention all the at-home and domestic support that set me up for success in running my law firm. Without my at-home support, there would be no way for me to be focused at work. Every CEO should have:

Housekeeper

This person or team of people does at least a weekly deep clean of your home. I know some people who have this person or team of people come twice a week. My favorite day to come home is the day the housekeeper has been there.

Executive assistant/personal assistant/house manager

This person manages everything on the home front based on the needs of the CEO and family, including email, travel, personal calendar, household tasks, and more. The role can vary, so it's important to think about what tasks that can be delegated take up a substantial part of your free time. I want to spend time on the weekends with family and friends, engaging in self-care, exercise, things that fill up my cup.

Nanny

As a woman with children and a working spouse, I understand the challenges of balancing work and family responsibilities. Having a nanny can be a compassionate solution that allows you to focus on your career while still being present for your family. A nanny can offer support and allow you to show up as your best self, rather than feeling overwhelmed and pulled in many directions. It's important to live on your own terms and do what's right for you and your family, despite societal expectations. As a mother, I believe that when my children see me pursue my passions and reach my full potential, that may inspire them to do the same. By running my law firm like a business, I have more freedom to attend my children's activities and spend quality time with them. I hope to show my children that it's possible to chase your dreams and be a devoted parent.

Personal trainer

Your health is your greatest asset. Consider hiring a fitness trainer to help you maintain and improve your health. A good trainer can help you identify areas where you may be falling short, such as nutrition, vitamins, weightlifting, and bloodwork. Taking your health seriously can extend your lifespan and improve your overall well-being.

Coaches and mentors

Seek out mentors and coaches who have achieved what you want to achieve, as they can be instrumental in your success. My own success is built on the guidance of those who came before me. To attract great mentors and coaches, demonstrate your own value by actively listening and seeking to help them. I've found that connecting my mentors with others who can help them is a great way to build relationships. These key relationships can change the trajectory of your career, opening up new opportunities. Give freely to those around you, and the world will open up to you.

Allison Williams

One of the most traumatic events in my life was firing my first office manager. She was the first person I hired as a solo law firm owner, and she had become a friend, adviser, and effectively a caregiver. Realizing that she could not keep up with the demands of the role as the firm was growing, I made the mistake of first demoting her to senior paralegal as we searched for another professional to be our office manager. This was emotionally crippling for her, caustic to our culture, and ultimately more damaging than if I had just ripped off the Band-Aid and asked her to leave.

But from the ashes of this dumpster fire, a prolonged suffering rose—one of the best decisions I ever made as a law firm CEO. The firm was up four attorneys, two paralegals, one marketing assistant, and one receptionist/file clerk, and I was looking for an office manager for the company. I ultimately up-leveled and hired an office administrator who had previously managed law firms of more than twenty lawyers. I paid nearly twice the salary of my first office manager, but in return, I received four times the productivity. She had answers to questions I didn't even know to ask. This was my first taste of having a true thinker/strategist in the company other than myself.

Every CEO needs a high-level second-in-command. Call it a COO, an office administrator, an ombudsman ... You need someone who thinks at and beyond your level to truly bring your vision into being. Without it, your vision can only grow as far as you have, which is fine if you are willing to stunt your growth to step down into day-to-day operations or continually struggle to bounce between daily operations and vision-casting work. I presume you do not want that struggle or you would not be reading this book.

Beyond your second-in-command, there are some mission-critical roles needed for every CEO of thriving, growing law firm. First, you need a chief financial officer (CFO), whether fractional or, eventually, in-house. This isn't someone to "pay the bills," though you may start with a blended role of finance manager—someone who handles accounts payable, accounts receivable, collections policy and practice, budgeting, and forecasting.

You will also need a "people person." This person handles human resources—compliance, annual and biannual reviews, performance improvement plans, etc. More than that, this person is your eyes and ears in the firm. As the firm grows, you will need a trusted person who is both a liaison between you and your team (so that you do not face chronic interruptions with day-to-day activity), and so that challenging topics can be addressed within the firm unhampered by the overriding fear that most employees have of upsetting their boss and jeopardizing their employment.

The major mistake I made in hiring my office administrator was in giving her all of the above roles. We definitely felt the impact of that mistake repeatedly as the firm grew, but in the short run, this strategic hire paid for itself many times over in the first year. Specifically, in the first six months of the year, the firm grossed $500,000. But in the second six months of the year, the firm grossed $1 million. We literally doubled our revenue in six months by adding the right strategic hire.

One of the greatest challenges law firm owners face when adding mission-critical folks is being willing to pay for them. Lawyers are a notoriously conservative lot of folks. So trying to convince a law firm owner to pay, at minimum, a six-figure salary (and often much more) to secure another version of themselves is pretty damn challenging. I certainly was no exception to the rule.

That is why the next strategic hire should precede all others—it is a business coach (or coaches). One might posit that I am somewhat biased because I am the CEO of a lawyer coaching company; however, the proof is in the pudding. Not only does my company coach lawyers around the country, but I personally believe in coaching to such a degree that I have business coaches for each of my three businesses, plus a life coach .

A coach is not someone who simply tells you what to do or copies and pastes the tips and tricks you can download from the internet. A coach is at once strategist, counselor (excluding in the area of mental health), adviser, facilitator, and, most importantly, the person who has seen and overseen the successful implementation of the strategies you are considering. Because of this experience, they can help you summon the intestinal fortitude to spend money when you don't want to, to have difficult conversations, to reach beyond your current mindset, and more.

Assembling the dream team of support in your business will skyrocket it to the next level. But you must always remember that you are the center of your universe. The quality of the business you create is singularly tied to the quality of business owner you become. You cannot create an A+ organization with D+ communication skills, C- emotional intelligence, and B- dedication. If you are not willing to stay the course when it gets scary—when you run out of cash, when you face emotional challenges in life, when people you love need more attention than you have time to give—you will never create a business that runs without you. Seeking solutions to problems is the only way to stop problems from thwarting your success—and why it is imperative to #NeverStopGrowing.

Billie Tarascio

Once we hit thirty people, it was clear we were woefully understaffed in terms of support. Every department needed more help. I had focused mostly on operations and severely neglected the departments in my firm that didn't bring in money. But to scale and eliminate the chaos, I needed departments and managers. I tried to find a number two who would help me run it all, but instead I've found success with a team of six managers. Six managers may seem like a lot, but Modern Law has never run more smoothly, and spreading the work across seven leaders means no one is overburdened.

Human Resources

I wish I had hired a full-time HR person when we were hiring 10 people a year. Instead, I waited until we were hiring 20 people a year or more. Our HR person handles performance, oversight, onboarding, and off-boarding, holding managers accountable. She runs committees. She is a resource for the employees and looks out for the best interest of the company. She's in charge of training and making sure that Trainual, our online training program, is up-to-date. She creates forms and processes and runs payroll. She helps with the hiring process by screening candidates, scheduling interviews, and dealing with recruiters. It's a big job.

Our HR procedures needed the biggest overhaul. We were hiring people at least once a month and needed to lock down hiring and onboarding protocols. I initially tried hiring an outside person for this role, but it didn't work. I had someone in the firm who was interested, so we made a plan to transition her from paralegal to HR manager. She absolu
ely loves it and is crushing the position.

Finance

I am still responsible for finance, but I needed more help. I hired a full-time bookkeeper. With the six companies, SBA loans, commercial properties, and a lot of people spending money, I needed an in-house, real-time human managing the money. By $4 million, we were bleeding money from unused subscriptions and software. By drilling into the details, we have been able to save tens of thousands. We also added a billing resource manager. Her job is to keep trusts full and have financing resources available to help our clients find the money to pay for our services. This has done great things for our accounts receivable rate and has been a big help to our invoicing specialist.

Facilities/Tech

My longtime office manager was so over HR, she happily gave it up in favor of technology and facilities. She is tasked with all computer setup, supplies, facilities remodels, technology upgrades for remote work, and technology project-built outs. She also oversees the billing department and in-house bookkeeper.

Marketing

We run our marketing in-house, and marketing is my baby. But a manager keeps things on track. She oversees our social media, SEO, and podcast people. She fields vendor calls and requests, has a hand in intake, runs events, and manages our Facebook group. She also works with HR on our internal marketing and communications initiative. When we got big and dispersed, we did not have adequate channels for internal communication. We have now developed committees, town hall meetings, and monthly internal newsletters to communicate which positions are open, who is coming and going, and policy changes, and as a way to celebrate employees of the month, etc. We needed to start acting like the large organization we were. The marketing team has its own weekly meetings, quarterly retreats, and rocks. It has its own bonus structure, budgets, and metrics for success.

Operations

We have three operations managers: two lawyers and one paralegal. We have tried having one attorney manager, but it was impossible. They couldn't manage a caseload as well as the demands of training and oversight for all the attorneys. With two attorney managers, each person manages no more than six people. The operations managers handle the training, mentoring, and oversight of the lawyers and legal paraprofessionals (LPs). LPs are a new class of practitioner unique to Arizona and we have several LPs who were longtime paralegals and are now licensed to practice law. They need significant training and oversight. Our paralegal manager manages the paralegals and helps quarterback work, delegating and making sure everyone has what they need to stay on track.

Accountability to metrics of production is key with this many people in a remote environment. Having a management team that knows exactly what the expectations are has made holding people accountable easier. Those who won't be held accountable have opted out. While this absolutely meant turnover, it was necessary to build the team and firm we have today—one that has a culture of consistency, accountability and excellence.

Everyone above is my leadership team. The most important thing is that this team is not divided. There is no competition or conflict of philosophies. We let the values of the firm lead and drive the decisions we make. I am incredibly grateful for this team. My job was impossible without them. Everyone is full-time. I know there are some CEOs who have part-time people in these positions.

The success of Modern Law can be attributed to the recognition that the firm was woefully understaffed and needed a leadership team. Initially, the focus was primarily on operations, but it became clear that each department required more support. A team of six managers, a full-time HR person, a bookkeeper, and a billing resource manager were added to assist with the various needs of the firm. The addition of the leadership team made it possible to manage the workload for each manager, hold employees accountable, and create a culture of consistency and excellence. Through effective communication and alignment with the firm's values, the leadership team has been able to work together cohesively, resulting in the smooth running of the firm. The success of Modern Law serves as an example of the importance of having a strong leadership team and providing adequate support to all departments to ensure the success of an organization.

Seth Price

The team that will build and grow with you is of utmost importance in your entrepreneurial journey. That team will likely start out with a right-hand person who helps you with everything thrown your way. Over time, each skill set is categorized under departments run by different people and, eventually, different teams. These departments include intake, case management, legal substance, accounting, collections, and marketing.

For a consumer-facing firm, intake is a constant struggle. When building staff in a personal injury practice, for example, many people will be coming in, interacting with case files, and communicating with clients. Each of those people needs leadership, often from the lawyer supervising the case. However, there are elements of cases that will require oversight beyond what that lawyer can accomplish while managing their legal workload. We see this in big law firms with different leadership structures for lawyers and non-lawyers; while lawyers can supervise the rest of the staff in most situations, there are certain issues that can be resolved by non-legal employees. Similarly, it may be best in some scenarios for clients to interface with non-lawyers. Both types of people are necessary for building your law firm.

One of the greatest moments in seeing a firm scale is the addition of an operations manager. Whether this person starts off as an office manager or comes in laterally, they are critical in allowing the law firm to grow. First, the operations manager frees up the owner from tasks like buying copier paper or ordering lunches; eventually, this role is solidified and builds into a COO position. This is when true law firm growth can happen. The legal operations position is what takes your firm beyond the scale of a large solo practice, allowing for leadership in the departments besides just the founding attorneys. As operations are put into place, each department benefits from the checks and balances of an organized, unified system.

The office manager, operations director, or COO can take much of the weight off the founding lawyer. It's a huge relief knowing that you don't have to answer every phone call when you're away from the office because you know each call is being screened by someone you trust, someone who knows what needs to get to you and what can be handled by other people. Personally, I had a magic moment in finding my first solid operations director. Being able to check in daily and get a summary of what I needed to know, trusting that I would be messaged if anything important came up, and knowing that things were being taken care of while I was away—these things are priceless to a CEO.

So much of a law firm's growth occurs in operations, management, and hiring. Many lawyers run into issues in the hiring process because they fail to build their practice from a business point of view. Most law firm owners are comfortable with business-to-consumer (B2C) operations—they know how to bring in clients and build a name within that B2C space. However, there are benefits to thinking about growing and scaling a firm as a business-to-business endeavor. Hiring an employee, for instance, is more complicated than a simple transaction between an attorney and a client. Unlike the somewhat straightforward goal of attracting clients, hiring requires an assessment of the candidate, their skills, and their personality, as well as your firm and its needs.

If you manage your staffing sensibly, you will see holes in your company organization chart as you build and grow the firm. It's valuable to leave open spaces on an org chart and say to yourself, "This is what I want to build and grow into when I reach X goal or Y amount of revenue." Setting these steps allows you to clearly see what you need to get to the next level. As intake scales and each department grows to keep up, you will no longer know every level of your firm as intimately as you once did. Make sure to begin scaling at the management level, allowing multiple employees to supervise smaller groups of people. Not only does this ensure the workload is manageable and evenly distributed; it also gives more employees an opportunity to build their talents. When you do have turnover, you have people ready to step into those positions internally.

Once you identify your personnel needs, the challenge is figuring out when to bring these people on. You need to think about building your practice from an employment law point of view to anticipate and prevent the many ethical, financial, and legal issues that could bring you down. You must also consider the dynamics of your current team and how potential hires will fit in, not just skills-wise but socially. For example, I have practice groups with one or two lawyers in them. Finding someone who fits with a set system is no easy feat, despite the amount of up-and-coming talent available. One employee is going to want to be on their own, another wants constant collaboration, and yet another wants to govern.

To find the right match for any given role, you need a large enough pool. Every once in a while, you get lucky and stumble upon someone great who sticks with you. However, the finding new talent, especially as you scale and begin hiring in greater numbers, becomes more and more difficult. What you need to build out your team will continue to evolve based on your firm's stage in the growth process. Your needs will also depend on other factors, like how you are leveraging the tools and technology at your disposal. Each stage brings new boxes to check and a greater number of personalities to consider when looking at potential hires. It can be easy to get bogged down by the details of it all, but it is crucial for CEOs to stay focused on the greater picture. The people you hire should align with your long-term vision for the firm's growth—this is more important than whether they fit perfectly into the firm's social culture or have the exact skill set to fill your personnel gaps.

Sandy Van

Be selective in who you hire. "Hire slow, fire fast" is based on this idea. You will need all types of people to run your business. You're more likely to build a strong team if you take your time to hire right and get rid of those who don't work out. No one wants to hire the wrong person or keep someone who's not performing.

Think of your team as a toolbox. Each employee is a tool in that toolbox—a tool with specific purposes and skill sets. Virtual assistants, receptionists, managers, and other team members are the key to making sure your team can focus on their work rather than wasting time on mundane tasks. Virtual assistants can get you started. They can handle tasks such as simple drafting and filing. They bill as a contractor by the hour, so you avoid paying many of the expenses that come with an in-house employee.

Your law practice will greatly benefit from having law clerks, and this will give you and the law clerks you recruit the chance to gain knowledge from one another. Law clerks can assist with writing activities such as motions, blogs, and related work. They will learn about the operations of a law firm and the areas of law you practice. Allowing students and recent graduates to serve as your clerks will give you both the opportunity to assess whether they would be a good fit for your team after they pass the bar exam.

To build a successful business, it is important to instill confidence in your employees. Someone who is self-assured and confident in their abilities will be more likely to take on challenges and drive the business forward. Confident employees can develop innovative solutions to problems that you, as a business owner, may not have thought of. As you begin to grow and cultivate your office culture, invest in your employees' development. I regularly bring my team members to conferences so they can learn about running a law firm, litigation, or the best personal injury practices.

Identify your own personal board of directors who will provide reliable advice and support. Find a banker or lender who will support you in your efforts. And don't be afraid to take out a loan if you believe in your business and its potential. The most successful entrepreneurs have used leverage to grow their businesses, just as Warren Buffet did. In his book *Snowball*, Buffet claimed that if there existed a slot machine that spat out three quarters for every quarter you put in, you would be inserting every quarter you had. Consider taking a loan and investing the entire amount in the "slot machine" that is your business. By following this advice, you will increase your chances of success in the long run. Remember, confidence is key when making business decisions, and leveraging resources can help take your business to the next level. Consider all professional recommendations, and trust your decisions and be confident in your abilities to manage your company's finances and business decisions.

A critical member on the board of directors is a mentor who can guide you through the ups and downs of entrepreneurship. This doesn't have to be an in-person relationship, and there are many resources available to you, such as books, courses, and virtual sessions offered by experts.

Investing in your own personal development is critical to your success. In developing your board of directors, take the time to interview as many people as possible, especially those with knowledge and experience in the area in which you are attempting to succeed. Learn from their successes and failures to avoid making the same mistakes. When you meet people at networking events or conferences, don't be afraid to speak up and ask questions. Some mentors sell courses on how to do things, and investing in these resources could provide a significant return on investment. Given the option, I would rather invest tens of thousands of dollars to accelerate my learning process than spend years figuring things out on my own. Having a mentor can help you avoid wasting time with trial and error, as they can share their own experiences and expertise.

Talk to people who have law firms. Open your mind to people who have successful businesses outside the legal field. This allows you to see things from a different perspective. How do they manage and grow their businesses? What skills do others use that you can apply to your field? Go to conferences and seek out these people. The speakers have something to teach, but so do those attending.

Dedicate time toward creating real relationships. View networking as planting seeds that, with time, will eventually blossom. This part takes patience, and you should not have any expectations. Nevertheless, show up, be yourself, share your knowledge, listen attentively to others, and be kind—over time, people will begin to gravitate toward you. Kindness goes a long way, and it has a significant impact on building lasting relationships. I make it a habit to connect with most people I meet on social media, which allows them to get a glimpse of my character. When people trust you, they are more likely to share information with you or introduce you to others. Use your contacts, especially at bar functions, to find lawyers or paralegals. Take each referral seriously. Hire experts and consultants when you can. Set aside your ego and admit to yourself that you don't know everything.

Allison McKeen

Ryan and I are big fans of *The Office*. If you haven't seen the series, one of the running jokes is that Michael Scott, the boss, desperately wants to be loved and accepted by his employees. But we all know that leadership roles are lonely. If you're implementing necessary changes and holding people accountable, some of your team members will not like it. That can sting.

Your mental health is critically important to the success of your firm. As CEO, you will need to find your emotional support system. Maybe that's friends you've met at a professional organization, a therapist, a significant other, and your dog. On days when you are struggling with the demands of leadership, these are the individuals who will remind you that you are so much more than the job you perform.

In the office, though, you should form a leadership dream team to support your vision.

Chief Operating (or Operations) Officer

The COO answers directly to the CEO and is responsible for implementing the CEO's vision for the firm. Basically, if a CEO and a COO were planning a vacation, the CEO would pick the location and the COO would plan the best way to get there.

When the leadership team sets a financial goal, the COO plots the road to reach that goal. This is the person who prioritizes hires and monitors firm data to watch for signs of problems. The COO would be the one to sound the alarm and present solutions if the firm is getting off-track. The COO is a problem-solver who understands the CEO's vision and knows the obstacles the business must overcome to realize it.

The leadership team may divide labor any number of ways. Our CEO (Ryan) still oversees marketing because he's great at it and it's a natural complement to his forward-facing role. But as the COO, I am responsible for overseeing all financial, personnel, IT, and regulatory matters. I'm the one who is responsible for making sure someone is answering our phones and our team members have the resources they need.

If you're not ready to hire a full-time COO, you might consider a fractional one. These professionals will cost less while easing the operational burden and helping your team stay focused on your vision.

Finance

Running a business—at least in Connecticut—is a regulatory headache. We have all kinds of tax reporting to do, notices to file with the town, and business license payments to make. We also have complicated state and federal laws and changes being made all the time. It's a lot.

When we started out, I handled this part of the business myself. I didn't have a caseload, and it's not terrible when you have three employees and one location. But at some point, these responsibilities become too much for any one person to manage.

Most of the lawyers I know really dislike the finance side of things, but mismanagement of client funds—even by accident—is the quickest way to get in trouble. One time our bank erroneously reported an overdraft in our client funds account, requiring me to write a lengthy letter to the grievance committee to prove that we *didn't* bounce a check. Until I received the notice that the investigation was closed, I was a mess—and this was for a false report!

Life is short. Get a bookkeeper and an accountant. This will save you time, money, and aggravation at tax time.

Personnel

One of our struggles as a growing firm has been managing employees. We used to all work together in one 1400-square-foot space. Now we are spread out in four offices across the state and working remotely all over the world. What I've learned is that if there are gaps in our communication, someone will fill in those gaps with gossip or complaints. It's very easy for a misunderstanding, often driven by fear, to take hold of a group of employees.

I wish I could say that we are always great at communication. While we try to be transparent, we sometimes don't realize how something might be perceived. A lunch for one group of paralegals (set up to introduce them to the new attorney who would be leading them) was viewed as a snub by another group. I don't want to know how many hours were wasted before we clarified the issue.

As you progress to CEO, you will create a distance between yourself and your team. It's just natural. But that doesn't mean you should allow this space to remain unfilled. Someone needs to be available to your team, constantly checking in with them to head off problems. This is where a middle manager can help, whether that person is a human resources professional or an office manager. If you haven't yet experienced time being wasted because someone is complaining they don't have the right keyboard, you will. And you will want to have someone there to deal with it quickly.

It's easy to carry too much responsibility. I fall into this trap myself. Your team and your clients will put as much weight on you as you will accept. If we feel numb with the pressures of the business, we can change that—it's *our* business. Push back. Say no. Ask for help. Hire better team members.

You got this.

Ryan McKeen

When to hire and who to hire are complicated questions for organizations of any size. They can be especially complicated for growing law firms who generally bootstrap their growth. This chapter doesn't map out every hire your organization will need. Every firm will be different in this regard. Rather it seeks to outline some key hires from outside the legal sphere that have made all of the difference for me.

To become a CEO, you will need to hire business professionals to support your legal professionals.

The First Hire

I have had the good fortune of coaching lawyers all over the world for the last few years. Most of these firms are six or less people in size. There's a reason they seek out coaching at exactly this point in their growth—it's when things start to get complicated.

Most firms start out as what I would call "a lawyer with help." That first hire is often a paralegal. Things are very simple at this point. All communication in the firm occurs between two people. Everything from office space to payroll is simple.

Soon, there is more work than there is time to do it. So a receptionist gets hired to do phones, mail, and errands, and perhaps to assist the paralegal. And then maybe a legal assistant to assist the paralegal. And then maybe an associate to help the lawyer.

And suddenly there are a lot of moving parts. Vacations have to be coordinated, systems have to be developed, and things start breaking. Firms at this stage have too many people doing too many things. Your paralegal suddenly finds themself doing administrative work.

Many firms never escape this stage. They exist in it, to some degree, in perpetuity. And that is fine. It is completely possible to make a good living with a firm this size. But that's not why you bought this book and made it this far.

You want to grow beyond this.

In order to do this, your fifth hire should be a full-time office administrator. This is a person who will free you from an ever-increasing administrative burden. They handle things like bill paying, facilities management, posting and screening job applications, and the million other problems that come up in the course of a day.

Paying this person, likely the first person you have hired in a non-delivery role, frees you up to do either more important work on the firm or higher-paying legal work.

Don't assume that your paralegal is the best person for this role. This may be a role you hire from outside the legal profession. You may want to look for someone who has retail or restaurant management experience.

And once you have filled this role, you will need to start looking for a director of operations and ultimately a COO, both of whom should have significant business operations experience.

Marketing

Marketing will always fall, to some degree, on the shoulders of the CEO. Even at the highest levels of business, this is part of what it means to lead a company. For example, Steve Jobs announced the iPhone. And with good reason: it is the CEO who is uniquely credentialed to speak to the market.

The inquiry shouldn't end there for you. In many small law firms, the CEO does almost all of the marketing with the help of vendors. That is unscalable.

I see firms spend lots of money on digital agencies, ads, and video production— as they should. You can realize great return here.

One of the best spends you can make is on an in-house marketing team. Your first hire can be someone who wears many hats—events, social, remarketing, and client experience. This is a smart marketing spend.

As you grow, you will need someone who can ultimately coordinate your marketing and interface with vendors. Next, you'll need someone who can direct your marketing as opposed to simply executing on your plans. If you scale large enough you will need a Chief Marketing Officer.

Hiring for marketing is a switch you must flip.

Finance and Data Analytics

There are endless business seminars on "knowing your numbers," and with good reason. Numbers are critical to any business.

Your finances are going to become very complicated. As you scale, your data is going to become even more complicated.

One of the more inspired hires that we made was looking at this as a "who" and not "how" problem. So we hired an accountant. We are now able to make decisions in all aspects of our business with clarity.

Being able to send a message asking about some data point and getting an accurate response frees me up to do important work.

IT Professional

We grew large without an IT team. And it was a mistake.

For years, I was our IT team, and it worked. Between all of our apps being best-in-class software-as-a-service programs and buying top-of-the-line MacBooks, it more or less worked.

As we grew, the demands on me and our office admin to troubleshoot apps, printers, and wi-fi became far too much.

Couple this with an ever-complicated cyber security landscape, remote work, and a workforce with varying degrees of tech competence, and getting professional IT help is necessary.

Human Resources

Hiring, onboarding, reviews, payroll, and benefits are also going to grow to a point that neither you nor an office administrator are going to be able to effectively handle.

Your firm will shift from need-based hiring to always hiring.

The sooner you can get a person with a background in human resources on your team the easier it will be to scale.

Resolving issues like conflicts between employees, keeping a finger on the pulse on your team, and keeping up-to-date with changes in the employment landscape will become a full-time job. This is a position that I wish we had hired sooner.

Michelle Dellino

You cannot do this all on your own. Well, you can try, but it won't go very well, and it's not sustainable. I know, I tried. From 2013-2019, I thought I could do it all. I was the managing attorney, the HR, the accounting, the sales and marketing, the intake, the operations, and—in my copious amounts of free time—I also practiced law with my own full caseload. It almost broke me mentally and physically. When I started to let go of some control, building a leadership team and putting trust in other people, I started to thrive personally and professionally in ways I could have never imagined.

Build an accountability chart and make a wish list of the seats you need to fill. When you have the chart and list, you can prioritize your hiring and your timeline. Just as you cannot do this all on your own, you cannot do it all at once. In 2009, I took a leap of faith and hired a COO who has been essential in helping me manage our growth, implement all the systems, do all the things that are non-legal, and basically keep me sane. Doing everything myself was killing my growth, even if I did not realize it. My COO is also my brother, so we trust each other with everything, and it was an ideal fit at an ideal time. Not everyone needs a COO, but you do need someone to assist with your operations and possibly even a part-time COO.

In 2021, I finally formed a leadership team. I wish I had done it earlier. My leadership team is me, my COO, my firm administrator, and my wellness coordinator. We have legal supervisor roles that report to us and attend leadership meetings monthly but do not hold seats on the team. Your structure may look different. To help you think about it, I will discuss the roles I think everyone needs in some form. How you structure is an individual choice, but these seats need to be filled one way or another.

HR

My firm sits at just above twenty people and has a full-time firm administrator handling human resources and other related issues. I wish I had made this hire at ten people, even if it had meant less profit for the firm and for me as the owner. When you get at or above ten people, you have ten different personalities, ten sets of needs, and a lot of internal discourse during the day-to-day between staff, leadership, and everyone in between. The amount of time I spent managing various HR functions and issues over the years myself, and then having my COO assist with management in recent years, has definitely cost more than hiring someone at ten people would have. Having someone in that seat to be the go-to for all things HR including benefits, training, compliance, and so forth is invaluable as you grow your business in a healthy way from the CEO seat.

Billing & Accounting

For most small to midsize firms, it makes sense to outsource your bookkeeping. Our bookkeeping team is a vendor who stays on top of expenses, gets me the monthly reports I need, and also handles check requests to be cut from the operating and trust accounts. This person/team should also be on the same page as your CPA and have deliverables throughout the year—quarterly, at a minimum—to help keep you, as the CEO and business owner, on track with your tax projections so you can properly forecast your budget.

Once you have moved beyond a handful of people, it likely makes sense for you to have an in-house billing specialist or accounts person. On our team, this person is our billing resources coordinator. She acts as the concierge and resource coordinator for our clients. She makes sure the trust accounts are full and that we don't have receivables. She works with clients on financing and third-party payer situations where a friend or family member is covering the cost of representation. She is the one our clients can come to if they have billing questions or problems. She serves as an important touch point for the legal team with keeping up-to-date with upcoming trial deposits and the needs of the client trust account based on the work. Our billing resources coordinator is a critical team member. We could manage this role without a dedicated person, but that would disservice the clients and be less productive for the firm. Earlier in the firm's growth, I was the person in this role.

That soon became conflicting and not cost-effective. Do yourself a favor and get yourself out of the nitty-gritty of this role early on by hiring someone else. We have almost no receivables because we have made this role a priority. You will never regret having someone to stay on top of keeping the cash flow moving.

The billing resources coordinator and bookkeeping team report to me and I essentially sit in the lead finance seat. Eventually as we scale past thirty team members, we will have a fractional CFO or possibly even a controller. I am evaluating options in the spirit of growth for now and see that happening within thirty-six months.

Marketing

You have to have a marketing team and a marketing plan. Once again, in the early years, this was just me. Later, as I truly became CEO and not just the "I do everything" person, I built my marketing team. Your team may not look like mine, but you do need one to carry out your plan. There is not a one-size-fits-all solution for the people you will need on your marketing team. As CEO, you first need to look at what you enjoy and what is important to you. You may want to hold a seat here, or you may not. For example, I enjoy marketing and sales. I spend a great deal of time on it, work closely with my intake team, and like sitting in what is essentially the CMO seat. My COO also has a strong marketing background and likes leading the intake team and working with me on marketing. I spend more time in marketing than many people in the CEO role might simply because I am passionate about it and have been since day one.

If you are not passionate about it, and you have more than ten people, you might consider a full- or even a part-time CMO to lead your marketing team. Our marketing team consists of two full-time in-house client liaison intake specialists, the COO, me, and also a virtual assistant behind the scenes who is fully dedicated to marketing. Down the line, we will be adding at least two more people to the marketing team, and I will likely step a little further back. But for now, I have the energy and time to spend here, and enjoy it. The most important takeaway from this should be to find what you enjoy doing and spend a little extra time there because your passion, creativity, and imprint will be felt by your staff and the clients, and it will serve your firm well. The same impact is felt when you spend too much time in a seat that you don't enjoy. Everyone knows when you're doing something you can't stand, when your energy is low, and it brings the entire team down. I suggest you work hard to identify what you don't want to do, delegate it down, trust people, and get out of the way.

The Legal Team

You are the CEO of a law firm. so that means the legal team is probably the first thing you think of when it comes to the people you will need. I elected to talk about some of the other roles first to help you realize that no matter how good your legal team is, you need a strong infrastructure of people supporting them. The support teams keep the firm running smoothly to allow the legal team to do what they do best, which is serve your clients well. The legal team should do a first-rate job serving your clients so they can bring in revenue to support the firm, keep clients happy, keep the referrals coming, and maintain a reputation in your legal community of excellence. The less non-legal work your attorneys do, the better from my perspective. I always bifurcate discussions about money and marketing from the job of the attorneys and paralegals so they can focus simply on their legal work. Many firms make attorneys into bill collectors and paralegals into intake people. This is not scalable or efficient. It does not serve your clients or your firm well. Let the legal team do the legal work.

You will need attorneys. How many depends on your particular vision, revenue, structure, and short-term and long-term goals. You will also need some kind of support staff. Some firms operate on a low support staff model, having the attorneys handle a larger book of administrative tasks than other firms. My firm has a full support team, with well-thought-out paralegal and attorney pairings to provide the attorneys the support they need and the paralegals a working environment that keeps them from becoming overburdened. You will also need to determine what structure you will use to manage the legal team and development. That may be one managing attorney, or it may be a combination of supervising attorneys and a supervising paralegal.

Getting the right people on your legal team is central to a healthy firm. Obviously they need to do quality work, but many people can be trained to draft motions and appear in court, have strong client service skills, and get the work done. You also need to be sure these people embody your values and they will be positive team members. Otherwise, they will leave too soon after you have invested significant amount of resources in them and will cause damage to your firm both while they are there and long after they are gone.

Tech Support

If you run a modern law practice, that means utilizing technology. Gone are the days of paper, binders, and needing to be in the office to do your work. If your firm is still practicing this way, you must change this because it's not sustainable, and everyone will pass you by. This means you need someone to help manage your technology. This is also not a one-size-fits-all solution. If you are on the larger end of a small firm, ten to fifteen or more, you may want an in-house solution. Perhaps someone on your team can sit in the technology seat, keep up with your hardware, inventory, software, rollout, implementation of software systems, security patches, onboarding and offboarding employees, and everything that goes with technology. In my firm, we outsource this to a vendor partner who provides ongoing tech support in real time, sets up and takes down computers for staff, and manages the security. Inside the firm, our COO manages our tech inventory, serves as the point of contact for our tech support vendor, and keeps things moving. As CEO, I have little to nothing to do with this part of operations, and that works well. This may or may not look different for you, but I would encourage you to figure out what your technology needs are, how you are going to stay ahead of them, and who would be the best person to implement them and provide support to your team. Nothing is worse than having multiple computers going down and no plan or tech support. Putting the right people in charge of this is critical for a firm to thrive.

Jay Ruane

When you run a service-based business, the biggest expense on your P&L will likely be your people, and picking the right people will be an important part of your success at the transition from legal entrepreneur to CEO. One of the biggest challenges I have faced myself is knowing when I should hire and when I should wait to hire. And I think this comes from a place of scarcity.

For years, I built my firm from a place of scarcity of resources. At first, it was a scarcity of clients and brand. Nobody knew who I was, and it took me a while to get clients. Once I got clients, I was still suffering from a scarcity of financial resources. No matter how much of my revenue I plowed back into my firm, there were always mouths to feed. And I needed to take some money home, too, because I was busting my ass, and having some money made it feel like it was worth the workload.

So scarcity has been in the back of my mind ever since I started scaling, and it has permeated many of the decisions I have made since becoming the CEO. It even has held me back, though I work daily on avoiding this scarcity mindset when making decisions for my firm because it can cloud your judgment tremendously. I have been slow to hire in critical positions, and that has hampered by ability to scale as fast as I could have.

So this chapter, for me anyway, is not going to be about who you should hire. It's going to focus on something you will need, and that are your "board of directors." Now, I am not suggesting you hire a literal board, but this journey for most of us is full of questions we have never encountered before, and your gut isn't always the best barometer of what the correct decision is. You see, many of us suffer from "déformation professionnelle," which is a tendency to process the world through one's professional eye rather than from a more balanced perspective. And to combat that, I would suggest you develop three people who you can run your ideas through so you can get some honest, critical feedback and also make sure you are not missing something. For me, those in that role are my coauthors Seth Price and Ryan McKeen. We talk daily, often by text message (although Seth loves to talk on the phone, and I haven't broken him of the habit of calling me... yet.) We run through scenarios, identify opportunities, and use each other as a sounding board for concepts we haven't fully framed out yet, which allows me to see the black parts I am missing in my considerations. I also have two others—Justin McShane, a criminal defense colleague who successfully navigated out of law to being CEO and who often steers me back from emotional decisions to data-driven decisions, and my personal trainer Rob Robriguez, who is also in a service business. We discuss my ideas, and he gives me feedback from a non-law consumer perspective.

All are critical to my success, and I rely on their brutal honesty with me to help me get to the goals I have set for myself, personal or professional.

One last thing about "The People You Will Need": you will need to replace yourself. And to be honest, it's not going to be cheap. The skills and knowledge you have came to you after decades of hard work and real-life adaptation to the needs of your business. You had no choice but to learn them. And so now you sit on the precipice of assuming the CEO role and replacing each of your skill sets. If you take $250,000 out of your firm and act as marketing manager, CFO, HR, and other roles, it could cost you 500,000 to replace yourself in each role, and your replacements may not even start with a full forty-hour-a-week position. Look to use outside vendors for some roles, and even offer part-time work for semi-retired or other professionals who may want less than full employment in these roles—but know where you lack drive and replace those roles first. You may *love*

HR tasks and doing your weekly and quarterly reviews. If you love this and hate the marketing weeds of A/B testing and developing an email newsletter, outsource the marketing role first. But don't hesitate to replace yourself, knowing it will cost you money up front, but the time you claw back and the personal time you get to enjoy will be worth it.

Bill Umansky

You are not an island. Although you started the law firm by yourself and your single-minded desire to build a great business, you will need an outstanding leadership team to drive your law firm forward. I will lay out the team I believe you will need to build and potentially scale your firm.

First, however, I would like to address a problem many law firm owners who are just starting out face when they are trying to build a team. They are undercapitalized. Most law firm owners quickly understand they need help running their firm. Naturally, the first person they will hire is the traditional law firm administrator. I also believe the firm administrator should be the first person you hire as part of your team if you have lawyers and paralegals doing the legal work. In many cases, due to economics, the law firm owner may elevate a trusted paralegal or legal assistant to that position. In the beginning, when you are small, that may work, but as you grow you may find that could ultimately be an obstruction to your overall growth. Typically, your first firm administrator will oversee everything in the firm including HR, payroll, finance, IT issues, software selection and implementation, marketing, sales, intake, collections, bookkeeping, operations, and training. In some cases, they are unfortunately still doing the legal work! While this could work short-term, it becomes quickly problematic if you are experiencing an explosion in growth. The firm administrator becomes bogged down and overloaded (even if they are a superstar), and they can ultimately have too much power in the firm and can become an obstruction to your ability to scale. This is because they don't have the capacity or ability to handle all those varied areas, but they may not want to relinquish control to anyone else.

If you are a small firm, you may be going through this ordeal right now. You may be stuck because you placed too much power in the hands of just one person and wondering how you can move forward despite the fact you feel very loyal to that person. Perhaps you don't have an administrator yet, and you are wondering who your first hire will be. In any case, you will need more than just a firm administrator if you plan to grow. You should start planning now for who you will need and making sure that your first leadership hire knows that they will have a team eventually who will take some of the responsibilities they may have now. If you currently have a firm administrator, then plan to get them to understand you will be taking away some key areas they control to give to someone else who can help when you elevate.

Who you need:

1. **Firm administrator**: An administrator can handle or oversee payroll, HR, hiring and firing, collection of outstanding fees, day-to-day finances, working with vendors, and handling any client complaints.

2. **Marketing director**: To have a successful law firm you need clients. You get clients by marketing to them. You will need someone to oversee marketing operations and make sure that you are putting out enough marketing and/or branded content

through various channels to attract clients. The marketing director can oversee several different departments, including:

- digital marketing (pay per click, search engine optimization, search engine marketing, local service ads, or any other digital channels)
- media buying (billboards, TV, radio, and other traditional means of advertising)
- social media management (ad buying, branding, video production and content, click funnels and more)
- production of an online and paper newsletter to be sent to former and existing clients

The marketing director could also be responsible for researching new channels to acquire cases. The marketing director must have the capacity to delegate and conduct an audit of the cost of acquisition of leads and clients, whether they're from paid advertising sources or even organic networking. Acquiring leads always has a price. It is important to determine what the law firm spend on that lead is going to be.

The marketing director can be creative, but in my opinion, is more important that they oversee the operations; the departments can be headed by creatives who market the law firm and brand in an effective artistic or creative way.

3. **Sales director**: you may have leads, but if you don't know how to intake them and, more importantly, close them, you will have no business. Having a sales and intake team is important, and having someone oversee the operation of that foundational part of your law firm infrastructure is critical. The sales director must be able to manage the circus. They must motivate, lead, manage, and understand their sales and intake team. The director of sales can train their team and make sure the team is

constantly motivated because without closers in your firm, you are doomed to failure.

Some law firms use non-lawyers to sell. The sales director must make sure that the non-lawyers are performing their jobs within state and local ethical guidelines. If the law firm is using attorneys to sell, the sales director should also be constantly training and evaluating the team. A good sales director will understand the KPIs and cost of acquisition because they will be evaluating the overall quality of the leads. While determining the ROI is the marketing department's responsibility, the sales director needs to understand what marketing channels are working—and if they're not working, the firm needs to find a resolution or move on from them. A good sales manager will be working hand in hand with the marketing director to make sure that qualified leads are coming into the firm and that the leads are being signed up.

4. **CFO**: Most lawyers do not have a business background, and fewer have a background in accounting or finance. Many lawyers rely upon their firm administrator or their accountant to give them financial advice regarding their law firm. This was a mistake that I made, and it was a critical one until I hired a CFO to really understand the data so I could make the appropriate financial decisions to move my firm forward. The CFO may work with your firm administrator or your leadership team to develop a budget. From that budget, they can then develop reports that will tell you about the overall health of your firm. The CFO can evaluate your team and their compensation and then develop payment structures to prevent overpaying or underpaying any team member. The CFO should work with the marketing department to evaluate whether the marketing director is spending money in the appropriate places to earn a return. An

additional role of the CFO is to work with your accountant to determine whether you are making the best use of your tax exemptions and to create investment and retirement vehicles. With these tools, you can put your money to good use for your law firm, including reinvestment, retirement, and taking care of your physical infrastructure.

5. **Chief of operations**: A COO is needed to oversee the operations and training of the different departments in your firm. Without proper and consistent training in place, employees will never move forward. If you do not have proper training, then you cannot keep resistance standards in your law firm through the natural progression of hiring, firing, and resignations. The COO oversees the creation and implementation of training programs for the different departments in your law firm. They are responsible for making sure that your legal and non-legal teams are running efficiently and ensuring training is put into place to bring new team members up to speed. They are also responsible for identifying where the breakdowns in your business happen. In our firm, the CEO usually receives reports from department leads when they can not resolve a problem in the department. The COO will then attempt to resolve those issues or will bring them up to a leadership team meeting so they can be viewed from many different perspectives and then resolved.

6. **Integrator or CEO**: We use the Entrepreneurial Operating System (EOS) in our office. The person responsible for running our law firm is called, in EOS language, the Integrator. The Integrator is the one responsible for overseeing all departments, including even the COO. The main responsibility of the Integrator is to remove roadblocks from individual departments and to motivate the leaders to find resolutions to difficult day-to-day

issues. They are the ultimate leader and keep the different departments working as a team to move the law firm forward. The Integrator is the bridge between the various department heads and the leaders on your management team and will ultimately run your leadership team.

7. **Executive assistant** and maybe personal assistant: While the Integrator/CEO may be the most important part of your leadership team, you will need an executive assistant who can assist you many personal things you do to move your business forward. Your executive assistant guards your time religiously, sets meetings for you, and helps you build on your existing relationships and develop new ones you are creating. They can protect your time from unwanted proposals and can arrange your business events and even throw them! They are an extension of you. They can assist you with gift giving, writing thank-you notes, and all sorts of other things. An outstanding executive assistant will be the master of your calendar. Often they will be the one telling what you need to know for an upcoming meeting and where you will need to be. A great executive assistant runs YOU!

8. **Business coach**: While a business coach is not part of your team on a daily basis, you need an outside objective person who can give you advice that's not tainted by money or position in your firm. They can help you develop values and goals for your firm and help you keep setting more objectives on a quarterly and annual basis.

9. **YOU**: You founded the firm, and now perhaps you have all the people in place above to help run it. So, what is your position? In my opinion, you should be spending 100 percent of your time doing what you love to do to benefit the law firm. If you are a visionary like me, you will want to be constantly creating new ideas. Since you would run your team by committee, you will

need to get approval and vetting from your leadership team. If you love developing business, then you go out and develop business. Do what you love, but try to ask the question *Does it benefit my team and my law firm?* If it doesn't, then don't do it, because people are relying upon you. Encourage your leaders, your other employees, your clients and vendors. Be the coach, cheerleader and the person with the optimistic "can-do" attitude.

Joey Vitale

Let's talk about your team. If you're like most law firm owners I know (and really, most business owners in general), there are two huge mistakes you're making that cause lots of problems within your team.

The first mistake is this: you don't have a team chart. It's very difficult, if not impossible, to get clear on who is doing what without a team chart.

Now, you might already have a team chart. But is it clear and complete? If not, then you're making the second big mistake. While having some kind of team chart is better than nothing, it is not clear and complete unless it identifies all the roles in your firm. It must also indicate who is responsible for which roles.

No matter what your team size is, even if you're a true solo, there are four key roles in your firm. Your team chart should include all four of these roles.

The Doer Role

The first role, and by far the most common one, is that of the doer. Your firm as a whole is likely spending 80 percent of its time on doer work. Doer work includes administrative tasks, client work, networking, and everything in between.

Chances are you currently own a lot of doer work that is well below your hourly rate. I'm all for delegating, but I encourage you to first delegate those $15-per-hour tasks that are eating up your time. Managing your email, answering customer support questions, repurposing content—a lot of tasks like that can be done well by an administrative assistant, in the United States or overseas.

So do yourself, your business, and your expenses a favor by building an administrative team that can handle those tasks like ninjas. Then, over time, delegate and outsource the more valuable doer work off your plate.

One quick note here. As you read this, you may be dreaming of a day where you let go of all the doer work in your firm. On the other hand, you might want to keep certain doer work for yourself no matter how big your firm gets. Neither option is necessarily the "better" path. Just get clear for yourself which high-value doer work—if any—you will want to hold on to as you scale.

The Manager Role

One level up, you have the role of managers. While managers aren't doing the doer work, they are managing tasks and projects to ensure that work gets completed. Managers are the ones who take ownership for the work getting done—and done correctly. They are responsible for setting priorities, delegating tasks, and monitoring progress. The better your systems and processes are, the easier and more fulfilling it becomes for someone to manage.

Let me ask you a question: if your team is just other doers, how long can you step away from the firm? Probably only a few days max, because all of those doers are reporting to you!

I often see so much potential for promoting existing teammates into management roles, especially since hiring external managers can get expensive fast. If you have a growing number of assistants handling administrative tasks, consider elevating one of those rock stars to a position where they are managing their administrative teammates. In fact, all of the managers on my team are overseas staff who proved themselves to be great managers.

The Leader Role

At the next level, you have leaders. Whereas managers manage tasks, leaders lead people. Your leaders are in charge of overseeing your departments. They help the CEO identify, plan, and execute on the firm's quarterly goals in order to stay on track with the bigger mission. If there is a serious problem in a department, it is the leader's responsibility to ring those alarm bells to the CEO.

Your leaders help maintain a positive work culture. It's vital that your leaders embody your company's core values so that they can empower the rest of your managers and doers to do the same.

You may be asking yourself, "If leaders lead departments, how many departments should my firm have?" I recommend the following: if you are currently the only person on your team filling a leadership role, then start out with just three departments: growth, operations, and fulfillment. As other teammates fill leadership roles, feel free to increase the departments. For example, you could separate the growth department into a sales department and a marketing department.

The Visionary Role

At the highest level is the visionary role, otherwise known as the CEO seat. In order to maximize your firm's growth, you must spend more and more time in the visionary role. Your time in the role of the visionary is spent coming up with ideas, supplying creativity and problem-solving at the macro level, cultivating big relationships, and improving the firm's culture, mission, and vision.

I like to explain it this way. My leadership team runs the business in the current quarter we are in, while I as the visionary work on business opportunities ninety days out and beyond.

If you're like most business owners, you may find it difficult to let go of these doer, manager, and leader roles. It can be tempting to try to do everything yourself. Resist that temptation, as it will ultimately hold you back. Trust your team and empower them to take on more responsibility. Remember: the more your business depends on you, the less it is worth.

Putting It All Together

You may have heard of team charts called organization charts (which are organized by individuals) or accountability charts (which are organized by roles). While accountability charts are the better option between the two, most accountability charts don't show the manager and doer roles within your firm.

CHAPTER 4

The Tools You Will Need

Billie Tarascio

Law firm tools come down to systems and software. There is so much that can be said about how to create and document systems and how to evaluate and choose software but, in this chapter, I am going to focus on 1) how to get people to use and follow your systems and 2) how to evaluate and consolidate technology.

Systems Adoption and Oversight

What can you do if you are in a culture where people are not following the systems? By mid-2022, we had hired 20 people in a year and lost another ten to turnover. Only 20 percent of the team was following the systems. The results were disastrous. The lack of uniformity was wreaking havoc on the team. There were constant case emergencies instead of intentionally and proactively handling cases. Paralegals and lawyers were extremely frustrated with each other, and there was a lot of blame.

We knew that people were not following the systems and that the culture lacked accountability. We also knew that following systems is about building good habits. We knew that simply following the systems would solve many of the problems we were experiencing, but changing behavior—especially lawyer behavior—is really hard.

I know from being a parent that behavior modification is a science. You must choose one behavior to fix and reinforce the heck out of it before moving on to another behavior. To choose where to start, pick the ONE thing that, if done, would make all other things better. I picked our monthly client status memorandum (CSM), and it offers a great example of how you can get your team to follow your systems.

In the height of COVID, I began requiring lawyers to complete a monthly CSM. The CSM provided:

1. A factual case summary
2. The strategy as it evolved through the case
3. All of our filings and accomplishments to date
4. A section to discuss budget needs for the case

Sending it to the client each month ensured the legal team was on the same page as the client. It would also allow another lawyer or paralegal to step in if someone got sick or left the firm. I saw this document as solving SO many problems, better facilitating communication, a tool for managers to identify when cases were stuck, protecting the firm and the lawyer from bar complaints and malpractice. It was billable work! But I could not get people to do it.

First, the workflow needed to change. For every other document in the firm, paralegals started the document and tagged the attorney with a draft in box. We changed the system to mimic our other workflows. That helped a bit.

Next, it was clear we needed a better way to track when they were being completed and by who. We started with a spreadsheet but that wasn't working. My partner Chad built a database with reminders and a dashboard for the lawyers and managers. The reminders went to Slack and the number of overdue CSMs was reported automatically and publicly in Slack. That helped a lot.

Finally, we needed a consequence for not completing the CSMs. This was the hardest part for me and part of our overall discussion regarding accountability in the firm. Using our values as a guide, we created our nonnegotiables and performance metrics. One of those metrics was the completion of CSMs. The consequence for not completing the CSMs was that both the lawyer and the paralegal were required to work from an office from 8-5 Monday through Friday until there were no more than five overdue CSMs.

As we rolled out this requirement and the consequence for not completing the CSMs, we gave people a six-week runway to complete the existing CSMs. On the Friday before the due date, there were 167 overdue CSMs. People worked over the weekend to complete the documents. Everyone completed them except one attorney. Her manager informed her she would need to report to the office on Monday morning and work from the office until the CSMs were completed. She didn't show up. She was immediately fired. This attorney needed to go. There was no question she was checked out and a bad fit, but with all the turmoil it was important for management to get our stuff together before we started firing.

Now people complete their CSMs.

To get adoption and execution of our CSMs took:
1. a template
2. a workflow
3. software for tracking

4. management/oversight
5. a consequence

We do not have a consequence for failing to follow each individual policy, but we did develop expectations and a plan for when people were falling short of those expectations. This also meant developing management protocols, expectations, and tracking/reporting tools. I hope this example can offer some insight if you find yourself in a position where people aren't following the policies. The policy may need to be changed. The workflow may need to be developed or tweaked, and/or you may need software.

Choosing and Consolidating Software

In our expansion, we needed more tools. We added Culture Amp for managing one-on-ones and employee performance, Criteria Corp for preemployment testing, and Trainual to help with the high volume of training and onboarding. One piece of feedback we continued to get from the new hires was that we used "so many systems." They were not wrong. As we grew, we added. When we chose each software tool, it was the best option at the time, but at a certain point you will likely need to relook at your entire "tech stack" and evaluate its efficiency.

It's much simpler to add software for a new need or process than to change from one software to another. There is a significant cost to changing software. This decision should not be made likely. The new software must not just be better, it must be so much better that it is worth the disruption of the habits and workflow of your team. The benefits must also outweigh the pain of data migration. Software companies also continually overpromise and underdeliver. While we love some aspects of

Culture Amp, we HATE the lack of visibility for anyone who isn't a direct manager. Had we properly vetted it, we might not have selected the software. I highly recommend more than one person try each software. Insist you get a free trial or can play in the "sandbox" account before making a switch. I have done this recently with two different intake programs that did not meet my expectations or live up to their promises.

To evaluate our software and workflow, we developed a tech committee. The first charge for the committee was to list each software we use, what features we use and love, what features exist that we do not use, and the cost of the software, whether it be per user or firm-wide.

The list was long: forty-one different software subscriptions. There were some clear options to consolidate, and some that we had been paying for we weren't even using. Then we began to study our workflows and identify opportunities for consolidation or automation. This will be a LONG project, and we must move slowly and carefully. The larger your team, the more deliberate and careful you must be. If I could go back, I wish I had started this ongoing list of software when I started the firm. It could have identified opportunities and saved us money sooner.

Seth Price

The tools needed to level up your firm come in all different shapes and sizes. Your employees bring a lot to your toolbox, which we'll discuss more in the next chapter. Other tools come in the form of technology or leadership skill sets.

From a technological point of view, there are many considerations in determining what tools benefit your practice's specific needs. Take case management software, for instance. So many lawyers out there resist the technology and try to manage it all through their own spreadsheets. This is an example of where the right technological tools can take your firm exponentially further, and the sooner you learn to embrace the software, the greater the returns. This applies to software for everything from intake to case management to accounting. I recommend speaking to your peers about what they like and don't like in the software they use to get an idea of what might work for your firm.

Trying to get the right software is important, but keep in mind that your firm's needs will change over time. Your software's updates (or lack thereof) may determine whether those programs continue to benefit your practice. Know that many of the decisions you must make about your firm's software may not make a huge difference in the long run. It's how you use the technology that really counts toward your firm's growth. The programs available nowadays have so much bandwidth and capability that we generally barely scratch the surface when using them. When I first started practicing law, we purchased programs that came with updates every few years. Today, we license software that renews on a monthly basis. Although those expenses might be daunting to new legal entrepreneurs, the software far exceeds its monthly cost in value when used properly.

One of the most important considerations is ensuring your various programs and technological systems can communicate with one another. Often, software companies boast much greater integration capabilities than their programs actually have. The key is to be realistic about what your software is capable of and what should be covered by your employees. Listen to the opinions and concerns of the people who use the software. Invest in training to ensure your employees can leverage the capabilities of the software, at least to the degree that it serves your firm's goals and vision. Building out the software beyond the basics can be hugely beneficial in managing and growing your firm while freeing up personnel to do tasks requiring a human touch.

I remember first getting case management software and seeing the scary number associated with training my employees. One of the biggest mistakes I made was paying for employee training but failing to continue it after a year or so. At a young firm, you gain new faces all the time. Throwing new employees into the fire without proper software training will only hurt your firm as you build and grow. With consistent training and opportunities for feedback, you can expedite the process of learning, systematizing, and leveraging any new software. This is key in ensuring your clients are taken care of as you scale. As you cede control over cases to others at your firm, you need to give them the technological and educational tools to manage those clients effectively. On a greater scale, you need those technological tools to allow other rock stars in your firm to oversee the staff members managing cases. Smart growth is ensuring your staff has the tools—software, training, oversight, etc.—to continuously meet the client's needs as your firm scales.

There are many tools outside of case management and accounting that are necessary to build and grow the marketing side of your firm. Certain software programs can help you check ROI for marketing spending, for example, or assess your web properties for areas of growth. When it comes to the fundamentals of running your firm, though, the software for case management, intake, and accounting are the foundational building blocks for leveling up. Once you have systematized the tools on the client-facing side of your firm, you should consider services that affect your firm internally, such as communication platforms.

It is critical for a growing law firm to utilize software that ensures employee engagement. For example, there are various communication platforms aimed at gathering employee feedback, which is particularly beneficial for virtual or hybrid workforces. At both Price Benowitz and BluShark Digital, we've gotten valuable feedback through services that bridge the gap between leaders and their teams. From the leadership perspective, these tools are crucial to understanding what is happening within a team. Employee feedback allows leadership to take the pulse of the organization and to stay grounded and connected. For employees, these services provide a space to share their thoughts: what is great about their role, what challenges they are facing, what they are upset about, and what needs to be fixed. Tools that give your employees a voice are critical in facilitating streamlined communication from the top to bottom of your organization.

Another tool set to take your firm to the next level is one that has become increasingly popular within the legal sphere: social media. The lawyers who will succeed in the next decade are the ones focusing on building their brands where people meet. There are hundreds of legal entrepreneurs using social media to build their brands. Everyone wants to be the one lawyer in their community that people know and trust. By spending even just five minutes a day on social media marketing, you can engage with hundreds or thousands of people in your local community who need your services.

From social media to intake management software, the range of tools at your disposal is as diverse as the issues they aim to address. Different platforms have different learning curves, but every new system comes with a cost in the short term in exchange for long-term benefits. It may be tempting to avoid using a new technological platform or program based on the amount of time or resources it will take to implement. On the other end of the spectrum, you may fall into the trap of wanting to automate everything and leverage every single function offered by your software. Choose the tools that fit your vision; don't adapt your vision to avoid or overvalue certain tools.

Jenn Gore-Cuthbert

In today's fast-paced world, technology has become an essential part of running any business, including law firms. I have always viewed our firm as a technology-driven one. Utilizing technology could give us a competitive edge over law firms that are resistant to embracing it. Additionally, technology is often more reliable than staff due to the potential for human error. Our firm has become so intertwined with technology that it is difficult to separate what is not tech-driven from what is.

Back in 2018, we became a paperless firm by creating digital files. This made file access and storage easier and more secure. We also implemented CRM software to automate tasks and set reminders for each case. Creating manual reminders was proving to be ineffective. To this day, whenever new software or technology is released, I try to embrace it and imagine the leverage it could create for our firm. The truth is that you either adapt or die.

Over the years, I have also learned that two law firms could have the same tools or technology, but one has taken the time and resources to build out the tools and technology to their maximum potential, while the other has barely utilized any of the features. The two firms will experience different results with the technology. It is essential to be cautious about the advice you take from other law firms regarding their experiences with a particular software. Many law firms do not understand the time investment required to customize software for their firm. We have consistently hired consultants to help us build out our software, which saves time and keeps our staff engaged.

Here are some of the top basic technologies that all law firms should have:

Intake software: This software should automate tasks for your intake process. Ideally, when a potential client calls your firm, the lead should appear on the intake dashboard. Your intake staff should manage that lead and see where it came from. Automatic messages should be sent out to that potential client until the client is converted. Intake staff should follow up with the lead according to the intake sequence you have designed, and automated texts, emails, and other follow-up sequences should be supported by the software. Without this software, your staff will be chasing leads all over a variety of places and could easily miss one. You should also have software that records all inbound and outbound calls for auditing purposes and lead attribution.

Client relationship management (CRM) software: This software should orchestrate a client experience for your clients and staff. All general tasks that need to be completed on a file should be programmed in for each case. Reminders should be automatically sent to each staff member on the file. Staff should always enter detailed notes into the software so that in the event someone quits or is terminated, another person can pick up right where the last person left off. Important deadlines like the statute of limitations or other court dates should be calendared in as a backup reminder multiple times. Without this software, your staff is likely to miss follow-up communication, deadlines, and other important events in your clients' cases. One thing I would strongly recommend is to find CRM software that is designed and dedicated to your particular practice area.

File storage software: Some CRM software has digital file storage associated with it. Having digital files is important, but it's also crucial to have a backup in the event of file deletion. I would also recommend investing in software to protect your firm and having a specialist to manage your cyber security. And if your team is working remotely at all, I recommend using software to track your staff's productivity. . There is incredible software that will report back weekly if your team is working and whether they are at or below their capacity.

Marketing/content planning software: The marketing department should use various software to plan marketing content, automatically post content, etc. You should also utilize software to create, store, and repurpose your marketing content and ensure your brand guide for style, fonts, and voice is followed. You should also use newsletter software to build, cultivate, and continually market to your list of past clients, current clients, potential clients, referral partners, personal contacts, professional contacts, and beyond!

Financial management software: Law firms should have automated bookkeeping software to help track expenses and income and to capture, organize, and predict revenue and law firm financial goals. All law firms should have financial reports created monthly, quarterly, and annually. These reports can be created through financial software. Additionally, all law firms should also be utilizing positive pay software, which is an automated cash-management service that helps avoid fraudulent checks. Positive pay should be managed through your banking system. Personal injury firms and other firms that receive regular checks should have an on-site deposit machine and deposit software to deposit volumes of checks right at the law firm daily.

Hiring and recruiting software: This software makes it easier to place ads and screen potential candidates, as well as helping with hiring. Some software can help to onboard and manage the team members regarding the employee manual, PTO, time off requests, and employee reviews. Having software to manage these functions makes it a much more user-friendly experience for your staff.

Digital phone/team chat/zoom software: Phone systems now can be run on either a physical phone system or a digital app on your cell phone. These digital phones allow staff to work remotely without the hassle of moving their physical phone. We also utilize the chat features that these digital phones apps often come with. We have a general chat dialogue for the firm and then teams within the firm to communicate as people work remotely some or all of the time.

Digital dashboards: The entire law firm should operate using a comprehensive digital dashboard. This allows the owner and the leadership team to access a variety of metrics and easily determine whether the firm is on track to meet its monthly, quarterly, or annual goals. Supporting dashboards from each department should feed into this master dashboard. By developing this dashboard system as well as "flash reports" (which show high-level key data), I was able to take a two-month off-grid maternity leave, and the firm continued to grow and thrive.

Finally, technology is an ongoing evolution. I have not named specific software here because they continually evolve. What helped you get to one level might not take you to the next. Also, the more software you can get to work together or consolidate, the better.

Sandy Van

You should apply the first tools to yourself. Books are the key to getting started in almost anything. By reading books, you can turn decades into days. They give you knowledge of what entrepreneurs have gone through and what they had to overcome, and they provide experience that you can learn from. Don't waste time reinventing the wheel. Those who have gone before you have already experienced the trials and tribulations of building a business or law firm.

Find a source of inspiration, a muse, that motivates you to succeed. Your muse could be a supportive family member, a competitive rival, or even a patronizing ex. In my own experience, my ex-boyfriend served as my muse for a time. He condescendingly dismissed my aspirations and said I would never be as successful as he was at my age. I used his doubt as motivation to prove him wrong. Find something or someone who pushes you to achieve your goals.

At one point, I had a real estate agent as a partner in my company, but he proved to be a terrible business partner who mistreated my lenders and Realtors. One day, I asked him why I should continue to work so hard with him and receive only a portion of the real estate settlement when I could become a lawyer and earn that amount in a fraction of the time. I despised him and his behavior. However, my coach advised me that the best revenge is success. So I started my own firm, and now I hope that when he sees my building, he recognizes my name and knows that I have succeeded.

Having a coach will cut down on the learning curve, provide accountability, and expand your network. The right coach will save you so much time, and time is your most valuable resource. It can help you meet people who have similar goals and aspirations to improve themselves, and who may provide marketing and financial tips.

Attending conferences can prove to be highly advantageous because they offer a wealth of valuable information. It's important to view conferences as an ongoing learning opportunity rather than just a one-time visit. Identify individuals who are making significant strides in your field and follow their work. If you want to fully absorb new information, you may need to hear it several times. It's beneficial to attend conferences covering other fields, such as marketing or how to business management, as they can offer knowledge and techniques that can be applied to your firm. Putting this new information to use can lead to big returns on investment and provide opportunities to make new connections. I personally attend many conferences on marketing, advertising, social media, and case management software. Being able to see how entrepreneurs in other fields approach their businesses is both inspiring and invigorating.

Time is one of your most valuable tools. Stop being afraid to delegate; it's the only way things are going to get done. Use delegation to make time for your own tasks. Set blocks of time that are several hours long so you're not multitasking too much and splitting your attention.

A great time-management method is the Pomodoro method. It is a simple but effective way to manage your time and boost productivity by breaking down tasks into short, focused intervals, typically twenty-five minutes long, separated by short breaks. Choose the task you wish to complete, set a timer for twenty-five minutes, and work on the task until the timer goes off. Then take a five-minute break. After completing this cycle four times, take a longer break of 15-20 minutes. This method will help you avoid distractions, break large tasks into smaller, more manageable chunks, prioritize tasks, and manage your time more effectively. The other reason the Pomodoro method works is because of *primacy and recency*. The primacy and recency theory is a psychological phenomenon that explains the ways in which people remember information. The theory suggests that people are more likely to remember information that is presented first (the "primacy" effect) and information that is presented last (the "recency" effect).

Reports are crucial for keeping track of and measuring activities within your firm. We have specific metrics for reporting and measuring our employees' outputs specifically geared toward personal injury. They include reports on: (1) treatment and gaps in treatment; (2) physical therapy and chiropractic treatment/bill balances; (3) counters and negotiation status report; (4) case and task count report; (5) transfer to litigation status report; (6) call rail audit report; (7) medical record tracker; (8) settlements; (9) bad review case update; (10) demands; (11) pre-litigation audit; (12) litigation audit; (13) dropped cases report; (14) lifeblood; (15) communication; (16) sol within 150 days; (17) cases referred by outside attorneys; (18) lien case status report; (19) litigation referred-out cases; (20) pending UM/UIM status report; and (21) cases in Interpleader.

The Entrepreneurial Operating System (EOS) is a comprehensive system and tool that helps entrepreneurs and business leaders manage their organizations more effectively. It aligns business goals with those of employees, creating a shared sense of purpose that fosters accountability and discipline within the team. EOS is based on six key components: Vision, People, Data, Issues, Processes, and Traction. These components help entrepreneurs measure progress, plan for the future, and address challenges as they arise, enabling them to complete important projects within their organization. While EOS is a valuable tool, it's important to customize it to suit the specific needs of your business. EOS is flexible and adaptable and has been successfully implemented by thousands of companies around the world.

Bill Umansky

There are many tools necessary for success. However, in my humble opinion, the most important tool necessary for a law firm CEO is MINDSET! Without the right mindset, you will simply fail. You could have the best case-management system, intake software, accounting programs, social platforms, organic and paid digital, and referral network... but without mindset, you have nothing. My coauthors suggest some specific tools, but I prefer to talk to you about the mind and what I've learned that will help you develop the will to overcome.

I was blessed to have lots of cases and some rudimentary systems I put into place after attending an EMyth seminar from the book *The EMyth* by Michael Gerber. He taught me about the concept of an Entrepreneur and how important it was to have vision and systems in place to run your business. The most important thing Michael Gerber taught me was the myth that a lawyer can scale a law firm without taking themselves "out of the business" so they can work *on* the business. I learned that concept and began to work on the business, but I was still missing that "thing" to put it all together and grow. I just didn't have the mindset.

When things were running smoothly, I was confident and on top of the world. But you and I know life is not always that way. It's all about ups and downs, and so is your law firm. Business may decline, valued employees may leave, human resource issues raise their ugly heads, and each day could bring forward some trials or tribulations. Personally, I suffered from the worker-bee mentality laced with the middle-class complex. I simply thought that when things got tough, I had to take back the work to save the day so I wouldn't go broke. When winning, I would was a strong captain the ship of my firm, but when the waves and the swell came, I reverted back to panic.

You can't be a lion or a lioness in jungle of law firms or a shark in the seas if you are going to go react with abject fear when an emergency arises in your business. You must have the heart of an entrepreneur, the steely resolve of a warrior, and the resilience of a cat with nine lives. You must have the mindset. How did I get mine? And more importantly, how do you get yours?

For me, a good friend and big-time trial lawyer John Fischer referred me to Strategic Coach, an entrepreneurial coaching company that teaches you how to get your head straight about business. I spent more than two years traveling all over the United States learning concepts by Strategic Coach's brilliant founder, Dan Sullivan. I learned how to inculcate the heart of a lion or maybe better put, a Tiger! Dan Sullivan taught me a lot of things, but the most important to my mindset was a little book called *The Four C's Formula*. The four C's are words to describe the life cycle of a true entrepreneur. Basically, picture a circle or cycle with the words Commitment, Courage, Capacity, and Confidence, all with arrows pointing to and from each word in a wheel. Dan explains that the first step an entrepreneur takes is Commitment. He explains that a business owner has to commit to a decision, whether that's hiring more people, taking out loans, or anything else big you need to do with your business. You just have to decide you are committed. For example, you may choose to hire your first set of lawyers. Well, you put the ads out, interviewed the candidates, and hired them. So now what happens?

Well, that's when the second and most scary part of the entrepreneurs business cycle kicks in: Courage. You may say to yourself, "Can I bring in enough business to pay my attorneys?" or "Can I afford the temporary or maybe permanent hit in income while building this law firm?" or "Am I going to fail?" Hell, you may be thinking, "What IF I fail?" As you may see this is the core of the cycle. This is where you build the heart of a champion. As Winston Churchill famously said, "If you are going through hell, keep going!" A true entrepreneur has that courage, grit, and resolve to make it happen—to meet that commitment and drive the business forward, sometimes on sheer will. When that happens, you begin to see the fruits of the labor.

Dan's third piece of the puzzle is called Capacity. Once you have the courage to see it through and succeed, you then develop the capacity. For example, you now may have a full stable of lawyers, so you are able to handle even more work and more complex and lucrative cases, and your law firm can begin to grow. That, my friend, is when the magic happens. You begin to develop real Confidence, the type of confidence you will feel no matter how bad a storm may rock your ship. But even then, the mindset is not complete because it is a cycle. You are just not developing confidence to weather the storm of your business, but you are developing the confidence to make yet another commitment. This time, an even bigger and better commitment. In this way, you continue the Entrepreneur's cycle and continue to make decisions you have courage to see through so you can develop even more capacity to have the confidence to do it again and again. Now you have the manifest.

Next time you find your business stagnating, draw the cycle. The culprit could be that you will not make another commitment because of your fear or lack of courage.

In summation, I strongly believe you should develop that mindset before you buy all the other tools or make big decisions about growing your practice. In order to grow, you will need a team, and your team will need you to have the fortitude to see it through, follow that cycle, and continue to grow.

Mario Godoy

Growing your firm on your own terms requires that you know your personal, professional, and financial goals. Once you know these, then you will know exactly what your firm needs to provide for you to succeed. Then you can draw up a vision, mission, core values, business plan, and marketing plan.

I mention these items at the beginning because they are fundamental to achieving the firm of your dreams. There are also great coaches and books that can help you develop these plans. However, I want to talk about some other important things I learned as I grew my firm.

As a business owner, developing your emotional intelligence and your resilience is so important. When you get to work, you are not there to find love from your staff and to get your self-worth from your team. You're there as the cheerleader for the team, the coach for the team, and the vision driver for the team. You need to work on yourself first before you can give vision and drive and confidence to someone else.

Becoming a Better Manager

I became a better manager at work after I started coaching my kid's American Youth Soccer Organization league. You can't yell at seven-year-olds; I had to figure out ways to motivate kids and keep it fun for them while teaching them some skills and instilling a winning attitude in them. Somehow, they've gone seasons with only 1-2 losses. I keep the kids spread out and tell them to pass and move the ball. You can't make it too complicated. Repeat the same things, the basics, until they're instilled in them and become instinctive.

It's the same with a business: make sure everyone knows what is the mission, vision, and core values are.

I send a monthly memo to staff about those core values, and I know I've gotten through to them when I hear them saying the same words back to me, parroting me or even picking on me about what I do.

Jack Welch inspired me to write thank-you notes to staff members when I see them doing something right or doing something that exudes Godoy core values.

KISS: keep everything simple, on point, and interesting to motivate and build a winning attitude... It's the same for seven-year-olds and law firm staff.

Competing interests are a real thing, and everyone has them. But for all the team's differences, they have so much in common.

Mario-ism:
Accept the fact people have competing interests, but that if we reach that goal, everyone wins.

Play the Long Game

On my office wall, I have a 24-month calendar. I've laid out what we're going to do for the next two years. My business goals extend out five years into the future. I think the number-one lesson I learned in developing Godoy Law that I took with me when I started my second firm, Estate and Probate Legal Group, is learning how to play the long game, plan ahead, and stay on course.

Resilience and Fortitude

Growing two law firms during Covid taught me a lot. During that time period, you had to do what it took to get to the next day. I like to think that it started with a choice: I could either play to thrive, survive, or die. I chose to thrive. It didn't mean that I stopped being afraid, but I made a conscious choice to continue on in the face of adversity. If you had a business during Covid, those lessons are now etched into your soul.

That's resilience and fortitude:yYou may be experiencing adversity, but you can choose how you react to that adversity. In my home, I have a copy of the poem "Invictus" by William Henley as a reminder that "I am the master of my fate; I am the captain of my soul."

Mario-ism:

1. *Always think about the long game,*
2. *Be resilient, and*
3. *Always be working on developing your emotional intelligence.*

Leaders have to develop their emotional intelligence so they can handle issues with their team. As a lawyer, I deal directly with the firm's clients. But as CEO, I have to make sure my team members have the skills, the attitude, and the tools to help our clients.

Emotional intelligence is learning how to channel and manage your emotions in a positive way, not a destructive way.

EQ is a skill I and other business leaders need to develop and use to handle our business frustrations and team frustration in a constructive way. If I'm upset or stressed or frustrated with someone on the team, venting my emotions won't solve the problem. Leaders need understand their own and each team member's EQ so they can communicate in a way that gets the result they want—and not in a way that inflames an already problematic situation.

Learn to Harness Dynamic Tension

Through HTM, I was introduced to David Emeril's *The Power of TED*, which taught me to use dynamic tension to reach my goals.

The first part of using dynamic tension is to be honest with yourself about what you really want. Then you take a hard and honest look at where you actually stand today. Only then can you truly assess the gap between where you are and where you want to be.

Dynamic tension exists between where you are and where you want to be. You can release the tension by moving toward your goal or by changing your goal.

In the end, you are always an empowered individual that has a choice.

As a business owner, there is always a myriad of things that you can improve. I think it's important to be specific about the results that you want. You can then choose to focus on the things that will cause the result to show up. Often it starts with taking a baby step toward your goal.

Joey Vitale

Most law firm owners are constantly juggling all sorts of tasks. It can all get very overwhelming. Even as you're reading this, you may be feeling burned out and bogged down by the daily grind. That's why it's essential to have a strong set of tools to help you stay organized and focused.

I know the other incredible authors of this book are real masters at tools. And with technology advancing so quickly, the go-to tools I currently leverage might be outdated by the time you read this. So I'd like to approach this chapter from what I hope is a different but powerful perspective. One of the strongest sets of tools you will need are what I think of as "accountability" tools. These are tools that help you stay on track with your goals, priorities, and projects.

I can't tell you how often I get asked: "How do you plan your day to be so productive?" Well, I've learned that the most successful people plan their day according to their weekly plan, their week according to their monthly plan, their month according to their quarterly plan, and their quarter according to their one- to three-year vision.

Strategic Planning at the One- to Three-Year Level

In one of my favorite books, *Vivid Vision: A Remarkable Tool For Aligning Your Business Around a Shared Vision of the Future*, the author Cameron Herold underscores the power of creating your vision at the three-year level. Three years feels close enough but still far enough away to make anything happen.

When you think about three years from now, what do you really want for your business? For yourself? Your family? The world? Don't worry about being realistic. We're waving magic wands here. Anything is possible.

(And if you don't know what you want, head to the last chapter of this book to learn more on this topic from myself and the other authors in this book.)

Be careful not to borrow someone else's vision for success or to choose a path that's expected of you. Once your three-year vision has been clarified, what needs to happen in the next twelve months to keep you on track?

Strategic Planning at the Quarterly Level

There's something magical about quarters. Ninety days is often a perfect amount of time to accomplish a big goal or complete a large project.

At the quarterly level, one tool you can use is planning retreats with your leadership team. These retreats provide an opportunity to clarify your priorities and projects for the next ninety days. They allow you to take a step back from the day-to-day operations and focus on the bigger picture. You can also use this time to review progress, set new goals, and identify any challenges or obstacles that need to be addressed.

When it comes to quarterly strategic planning, no one does it better than my dear friend Melissa Shanahan. Through her company, Velocity Work, Melissa helps law firm owners get crystal clear on where they're going, take planning seriously, and honor their plans. Check out her amazing podcast and resources at www.velocitywork.com.

At my firm, we've developed an important rule: you can't pivot away from quarterly goals until the quarter ends. Why do we do this? Because there is a natural tendency as you work on a large project to start to lose confidence that it's the right goal. Maybe you realize your whole plan depended on a few assumptions that were off the mark. Maybe you come across a really great idea that seems way more effective than the goal you decided to commit to. Stay the course. Honor your plan.

Strategic Planning at the Monthly Level

Now that we've set our quarterly goals, we can spend our months taking action on those goals while getting other work done.

While you don't want to lose focus on your quarterly goals, you should keep a constant eye on how the firm is doing. Depending on certain numbers and metrics, you may need to alter your plans if something is off-track. At the monthly level, you can identify your sales goals, intake call goals, and other KPIs. These help you track your progress and ensure that you are on track to meet your objectives. You can use KPIs to measure success in areas such as marketing, sales, finance, systems, client matters, and your team.

Pro-tip: I know for a fact that all of the coauthors of this book are amazing at identifying, clarifying, and monitoring their KPIs. I bet they'd each jump at the opportunity to help you on this subject if you ask. I also encourage you to reach out to my dear friend and impressive firm owner, Christopher White. Chris is particularly adept at knowing his numbers, and he's one of the kindest and most generous lawyers I know. You can learn more about him and his firm at www.eques.law.

Strategic Planning at the Weekly Level

At the weekly level, I am a huge fan of weekly accountability calls. These calls allow you to brain dump everything that's on your mind, get tasks on your calendar, and move events on your calendar to minimize conflicts and maximize your effectiveness. These calls help you stay organized and focused on what needs to be done.

If you're just starting or are a true solo, you will likely start off by having these weekly accountability meetings by yourself. As soon as you can, consider adding a teammate to these meetings. An executive assistant is a great fit. It is much easier to "show up" for these meetings when someone else will be there. And they can help you stay focused on completing these steps every week.

Strategic Planning at the Daily Level

At a daily level, the most effective law firm owners honor what's on their calendar, batch their inbox review time, and do the important deep work without getting distracted.

Now, here's something that might surprise you (it definitely surprised me). When I learned to follow these strategic planning steps, I quickly discovered that I didn't need a to-do list anymore. Actually, it would be more accurate to say that my calendar is my to-do list. At a daily level, I simply follow my calendar.

In conclusion, these strategic planning "tools" will help you stay organized, focused, and accountable. By intentionally planning at the annual, quarterly, monthly, weekly, and daily levels, you can stay on track with your goals and priorities. Plus you'll ensure that you are making progress toward your objectives and in the right direction. This means you can effectively manage your time, stay focused, and turn your dreams into reality.

Allison Williams

Anyone who knows me now as the founder and CEO of Law Firm Mentor knows that we help solo and small law firm attorneys to "grow their revenues, crush chaos in business, and make more money." My instinct to crush chaos is very much derived from my personal experience of being exceptional at creating it!

Chaos comes when growth occurs unmanaged. Managing growth is one of the most challenging aspects of being a CEO, but it is also the most critical. So, how does one "manage growth"? I can certainly share with you a list of written procedures, technological devices, strategies, and tactics that would help you, too, manage business growth; however, the practicality of any given software or tool is dependent upon the law firm in which it is installed. The list of such tools is endless.

For now, I want to take a moment to share an overarching approach to systematizing your law business that will help you manage the growth and sustain profit in your firm overall. From there, I will share some insights as to what is most applicable to the role of law firm CEO.

Systems Approach > Any Given System

First, it is critical to understand that having a systems approach to business is the number-one way to reduce stress, increase efficiency and profitability, and exponentially increase satisfaction at work, including your own satisfaction. Getting your firm to a point where things happen automatically—through a system, with a designated responsible person assigned to handle every function of the business—is key.

Far too often, law firms are only as good as the quality of the employee doing a given task. That means that as soon as your favorite secretary goes on vacation, the quality of your business declines. To avoid this, you must have a designated person and coverage person for each function in the firm and a standard to which every person can be held accountable.

KPI Culture: Standards You Can Use

KPIs should drive your assessment of firm health. To manage by KPIs, you must have well-maintained data. Practice management software is vital. It must include reporting of detailed financial metrics, such as effective rates of your team, average case values of each matter, the average length of each case and stage of case, the dollars generated per billing professional, etc. This will give you significant ease in making decisions.

As CEO, three critical areas will remain under your direct oversight: leadership (visionary work), team/personnel, and financial allocation. There are specific tools you will need in each of these areas.

Leadership Tools

The most important tool you will need to possess, manage, and become intimately familiar with is your CEO schedule. This is not merely your calendar. Your CEO schedule should map out your priorities. Expect to spend your time throughout the entire year ahead in places intrinsically linked to your priorities. This should include:

- Start time of your day
- End time of your day
- Meetings with key team members, e.g., CFO, COO, CMO
- Marketing activities—speaking engagements; publication authorship
- Business travel—including staycations to work "on" the business
- Vision-casting retreats
- Conference attendance—CLEs and business-related
- Communications time
- Coaching/business mentorship
- "Office hours"
- Family time
- Personal vacations
- Self-care (exercise, medical care, mental health treatment/maintenance, etc.)

This schedule is your life success blueprint for the year. I typically spend the month of December of each year planning out my calendar of events for the following year.

The larger your firm, the more imperative it is that you guard your time. If you are not a structured person, you must learn the skill of blocking out "unavailable" time and allocating available time. This is not optional.

Team/Personnel Tools

As a CEO, your vision for the company is unique to you and cannot be delegated. Your vision must not only include what it looks like from the outside in, but also from the inside out. Firm culture is critical. While I recommend that all law firm owners use hiring assessments, the use of assessments in driving performance and cultivating leadership within your firm takes on greater significance as you begin developing leaders in the firm.

For hiring, I highly recommend using the Real Talent Hiring assessment—an extensive assessment tool that tells you information about how a candidate manages tasks, themselves, and others. There are many assessment tools one can use to determine work styles, conflict management strategies, and personal biases. For instance, knowing the DISC profile and the Myers Briggs personality type of those with whom you will work most closely is particularly beneficial.

For instance, I am an INTJ woman and I have a DC DISC profile. Because I am the greatest student of me, I am able to use these assessment results to educate all new hires on how I like information delivered, where I am strongest, where I am least likely to be effective, etc. Teaching others how to work best with you is an acknowledgment that a person entrusted to get things done alongside you must master the art of "managing you."

Financial Tools

One often overlooked area of concern in law firms is financial data management. It is not sufficient to hire an amazing finance manager, bookkeeper, and accountant. Nor is it sufficient to have a financial planner or benefits coordinator. As the CEO, you must be vigilant in overseeing the financial health of your company. This means becoming intimately in tune with your numbers, financial trends, and opportunities. Integrated dashboards help synthesize and communicate a snapshot of your financial data so that it is easily accessible.

Conclusion

Undoubtedly, there are countless tools you will need as a CEO. The list of software applications that can help you in this regard are too numerous to name, but the above provides a brief synopsis of the tools most pertinent to the role of CEO.

Elise Buie

- Mindset shift
- Authenticity
- Humility
- Confidence
- Empathy
- High energy
- Resilience
- Grit
- Resourcefulness
- Gratitude
- An open mind
- Growth mindset
- A great sense of humor
- Business acumen/business education
- Mentors/coaches
- Systems, systems, systems
- An efficient yet cost-effective, comprehensive tech stack (I'll let others talk to you about this)
- Financial controls
- Marketing strategy and execution
- High risk tolerance
- Leadership skills

My tools chapter has nothing to do with "regular" tools or tech—I will let my coauthors who are much more tech-savvy discuss the practical "tools" like practice management software,

CRM, communication tools, tech stacks, integrations, etc. My main tech tool is techy people who love Zapier and all things tech...

I would be remiss, however, if I did not mention ChatGPT and AI as tools that are barreling down on law firms and will change the firm landscape quickly as many owners deal with labor shortages and an increased need for marketing touches in the post-pandemic digital world. ChatGPT provides a frictionless entry point to any written word—it's a powerful time-saver for sure. Again, my coauthors are much more tech-savvy than I am and will likely have a lot more to say on this topic.

Now to the tools that matter most to me—mindset, mindset, mindset. Truly, mindset is everything. It creates either joy or dread. It determines whether I am succeeding or failing. It determines whether I have a great day or a horrible day. It dictates whether my team is succeeding or failing. It determines whether I am content or lacking. It's absolutely the most important tool I work with each and every day. Getting your mind right is the first step to your success as a CEO. I have fielded hundreds of calls and DMs from attorneys starting out on this CEO journey, and mindset is always front and center of the problems they describe. I cannot emphasize enough how important it is to wrangle your mindset—most importantly your ability to own your mistakes from a place of curiosity minus all defensiveness, eagerness to get candid feedback about faults and weaknesses, and a dedication to improving yourself. It is a humbling process, but it will fuel your ability to successfully lead others with a compassionate, servant heart. Truly losing your excuses helps you find results. Eagerly and quickly turning that mirror onto yourself propels your team's success. Allison

Williams, my coauthor and the Law Firm Mentor, was instrumental in helping me understand the massive mindset shifts I needed. She has been a wealth of mindset expertise and support over the last several years. Another great mentor has been Ryan McKeen, who is an amazingly humble, hard-working, servant leader who has consistently showed up each and every day to build his firm according to his core values.

I opened my virtual firm in 2015, way before remote work was "Covid cool." I knew when I started this office that I could not be chained to a desk in downtown Seattle each afternoon because 3-9 p.m. was my "Super-Charged Mom Time" for our large brood. The kids needed me to drive them to their various activities all over the city, to hear the ups and downs of their day, to be available for school things like science projects, and even some "New Math" tutoring over the years. We also prioritized eating together as a family each day, so there was shopping, cooking, eating, and cleaning. A virtual office allowed me and my team to work at the times that served our needs best. I often woke up at 3:00 a.m. and finished the bulk of my work by 3:00 p.m., meeting my family's needs as they arose during those hours but knowing that they had my undivided attention most days from 3-9 p.m. Now our virtual firm has about thirty-six employees and contractors all who work remotely on individualized schedules that meet their needs. It's the most amazing feeling knowing that I can provide unfettered flexibility to our team so that they, too, experience true life-work integration.

I have a few mindset hacks that serve me well every day in this CEO role. First, I luckily wake up happy each morning, ready to tackle the day. It does not matter what happened the day before; somehow sleep just turns on the happy part of my brain.

That optimism fuels me each day. When I do find myself stressed or anxious about something, I follow Dr. Jason Selk's advice from his book, *Relentless Solution Focus.* Ask yourself, "What is the one thing I can do in this moment to move this forward?" Simply by asking that one question, you take your mind from spiraling into anxiety to solution-focused; it is game-changing. You do that one thing, then ask the same question again and again. Next thing you know, your mind is solution-focused and you are humming along toward solutions rather than spiraling in "what ifs."

Another hack is my most recent "aha" moment, "Don't micromanage people. Instead, micromanage systems." Wow, I was mind-blown when I read this and absorbed the impact of this shift. When I am faced with a mistake or problem, instead of asking, "What happened?" with a person-focus, I now ask, "What system underlies this task?" Well, in many cases, as we collaborate on this answer, we realize there was either no system in place or the system was not used. Game-changing!!! Now, instead of playing the blame game, we are working together to fix our systems. A system-focus empowers the person who made the mistake to fix it and to empower others not to make the same mistake in the future.

My overarching mindset hack is that every problem my firm has can be traced back to me and something I am doing or not doing. As the leader, it is empowering to realize that all of the issues can be traced back to me in some way. Often I find that I have allowed or condoned certain behaviors or faulty systems that are creating our current issues. Because I can only change myself and my own actions in this life, this realization is quite empowering (once I get over my frustration that I have a new area of needed self-improvement).

Last, if I find myself stressed out and need to just "reboot" my brain, I take a "stress nap." I literally go curl up with a soft blanket and a kitty (I am a Hygge nut), turn on a guided meditation (try Claire Parsons' guided meditations on brilliantlegalmind.com) and sleep for a bit. Because of the first hack mentioned above, sleep creates happiness in me; I wake up happy, unstressed, and ready to tackle the problem again with a fresh mind and new ideas. And I actually add self-care and joy (2 distinct calendar entries) to my calendar each and every day. That looks like massages, hot tub soaks, reading, walks with Doug, a nap, kayaking, looking for Orcas, a dinner with friends, a zoom coffee with a colleague, Ted Lasso… you get the idea. Get to know your own brain and create mindset hacks that fuel your peace and success.

Coupled with mindset as the most important tool in my toolbox is authenticity. In order to successfully and sanely lead a law firm, you must be zeroed in on who you are at your core, what makes you tick, your deeply held core values, your zone of genius, your growth areas, your why, what makes you crazy, what energizes you, what drains you, what is soul-crushing to you, what tasks do you get lost in for hours… Once you authentically know yourself, you can hire around your weaknesses so that you can be your best self and work in your zone of genius. This knowledge also allows you to avoid decision fatigue; being so zeroed-in on your core values and your authenticity makes decision-making easy both for you and your team because there is little question about how you would handle a situation.

Embracing my authenticity was a bumpy process. After hiring several people in leadership positions who might be excellent in their roles with another CEO, I learned that the "Eeyores" of the world drain the life right out of me. I am absolutely a "Tigger" and need a certain level of energy around me in order to be my best self. When I am surrounded by Eeyores, I dim my own light, diminish my voice, hold back on ideas, and second-guess everything I think as I want to avoid their negative, ho-hum responses. These shrinking behaviors directly contradict my role as a visionary, so I now surround myself with growth-minded, high-energy people who see endless possibilities, not just barriers. Now, that does not mean that I don't need Eeyores on my team to do specific tasks—for example, a Tigger like me might need an Eeyore on the finance team to ensure that I don't spend all the money on my next wacky idea. But it does mean that I am not going to spend lots of 1:1 time with that person without preparing myself for their Eeyore vibe and reminding myself of their zone of genius. I likely won't bring my newest idea to that Eeyore alone. Knowing myself well helps me protect my emotional well-being and my joy.

Resourcefulness is another mindset hack that has paid dividends in my life. I firmly believe that every single problem, no matter how overwhelming it might seem in the moment, has a viable and, often, creative solution on the flip side (As Bill Umansky so eloquently says, "Flip that pancake.") For every threat identified in a SWOT analysis, there is an amazing opportunity. Creative problem-solving jazzes me so the inevitable grind of constant CEO problems actually challenges my brain and energizes my soul. I can't imagine what drudgery this CEO role would be if one viewed problems solely as obstacles. I think of problems as the "super-connector highway"—there is not a problem I face that is new to the world.

Therefore, when I am in problem-solving mode, I am often in "super connector" mode—looking for someone rather than some *thing*—someone who has faced and overcome a similar problem. Inspired by their past solutions and eager to creatively solve my problem in an authentic way, I seek out others to help me navigate my particular situation with the benefit of their lived experience. *Who Not How* by Dan Sullivan is a great read on this topic.

Financial controls—My 13-month forecast is my favorite financial tool. I use my financial forecast like a roadmap of all things—hiring, expenses, profit, growth, labor costs, ROI, productivity. I also have a competition with myself to see just how close I can come in actual numbers to the forecasted amount—my goal is less than a 2-percent variance. Some financial metrics that one must drill down on to create a sustainable business are: employee salaries as a percentage of revenue

1. ROI of employees
2. Profit per employee
3. Profit percentage each month
4. A/R
5. Expenses as a percentage of revenue
6. Cash flow

Knowing your numbers in exacting detail allows you to pull levers when needed rather than waiting on a month-end or quarter-end report. The point of this CEO gig is to create a business you love that fuels the life you love.

Jay Ruane

This is the chapter that I think a lot of people might turn to right away. Everyone is always looking for that holy grail of tools, apps, and "things" that would make running an actively scaling law firm easy. I don't have those answers for you. Everyone is forging their own path in their own way. And my tool set might not fit your needs. You may be crossing an ocean while I am hiking through a forest, if you know what I mean. But while every journey is different, there are some things you need to pack to survive, and I'd like to talk about some of those.

Your foundation will be a CRM. This can be anything from a spreadsheet to a tightly optimized digital platform. There are so many on the market that it's impossible for anyone to say which one is best. But in reality most of us scratch the surface of what some of these can do. In the end, you need to store your clients' data: name, email, contact info, and how you interacted with them. Focus on the system that gives you the best internal fluency. See which one feels most intuitive to use. Unless there is a feature you see in a new CRM that you cannot live without (and can't make work within your current system, stick with your current system—don't change CRM just because something is new and shiny. This wastes time and money. And remember, as you are scaling, you are also concerned about the adoption AND ADAPTATION rate of your team. Not everyone is interested in a new look and feel when the core functionality is the same. Involve your trusted team with this process if you are even considering a switch, and see if you can replicate functionality with a plug-in, add-on, or third-party service before you simply dump a CRM that is otherwise fine.

You see, one of the tools you need is the ability to distinguish signal from noise. The signal is the meaningful information that you're actually trying to detect. The noise is the random, unwanted variation or fluctuation that interferes with the signal. CRM companies (and virtually every vendor salesperson) are

GREAT at throwing up noise and highlighting the few signal pieces that might make them a little different. In my experience, if one of the commonly used platforms has a feature, the one you are on will add that within a year. Ask for it if it isn't announced. Emails and requests from enough customers asking for a feature can save you thousands of dollars and hours in switching.

For communication with clients, I would recommend a robust email marketing platform. Many have the same functions: email campaigns (like for automated drips or recurring newsletters) and some integrate sms into the feature set. In 2023, I would recommend avoiding a platform that doesn't allow for sms automation because text messages are one of the BEST ways to communicate with clients.

One of the other tools you need to develop is consistency. Just like you won't lift more weight if you don't consistently go to the gym and push yourself to get better, you won't see results without the tool of consistency. A single annual newsletter isn't worth much. A monthly is better, and a weekly could be ideal. But what I have found, even with myself, is that GREAT ideas that pay dividends can be abandoned not because of an informed decision, but because you fail to execute consistently. I have found that with consistency, my email newsletter gets opened by more people each month and the number of clients who consistently open it grows as well. This is allowing me to stay top of mind with them. Every year, around December, I look back on some of my greatest tools for growing my firm and realize that something that was working well was abandoned. For example, I developed a good name and buzz by shipping wine to every lawyer who was congratulated on my statewide criminal defense lawyers listserv when they won a trial. I did this for five years, and everywhere I went, I was approached by lawyers when I crossed paths with them in an outlying courthouse so they could thank me in person. People loved my "wine for winners" gifting, and it made me stand out. I abandoned it when Covid hit—no trials = no winners—and I realized just recently that I needed to bring it back because there was a new crop of lawyers winning cases who needed to know who I am. But going forward, I am removing myself from the day-to-day execution of this idea, making it easier to scale and maintain in perpetuity. I need to consistently maintain the things that work and not simply shift to the "new and shiny" because it is more exciting. That's the tool of consistency you will need to scale your firm.

Finally, a tool I could not have grown without was a willingness to dive deep into subject matters—both legal and non-legal. You see, not only did I focus on DUI science as a niche within criminal defense, spending hundreds of hours at seminars and trainings with the best of the best, I also spent hundreds of hours learning the components of marketing a service-based business. Too many times I sit with lawyers at seminars who tell me, I just want to step back and manage the marketing and have someone else run around and do the client work." Here is the problem with that approach. Have they studied effective landing pages for paid ads? Do they know how to write compelling drip campaigns? How about color theory and how it applies to website design? You can really squander great opportunities by thinking you know as much as a professional who has their career hanging in the balance when you hire them to execute for you, either in-house or a vendor. When you choose to undertake such work, you have to be honest with yourself and check your ego to see whether you want to "oversee the marketing" because it's more "fun" than law or *you can actually contribute to the process*. Dive in and get a true education on service marketing, and I am OK with it, but don't do it because you think it is more fun than practicing law. In that situation, you are not acting like an educated CEO making informed business decisions, but like a spoiled teenager who won't do what is necessary to succeed and thinks it will just come to them because they are owed it. And when you are educated about a subject, wow, you can REALLY engage with employees or vendors, offering your opinion backed up by fact, and you can scale so much faster.

Allison McKeen

The tools a CEO requires to be successful are really systems: automated systems, hiring systems, and operating systems. As you transition to CEO—even as you work as CEO—the question to ask yourself when confronted with a task is: is doing this the best use of my time, or can someone else do it?

This isn't because you're lazy but because your time is valuable and rare. As CEO, you are the only person in your firm who can complete crucial leadership duties. So if someone else can perform a task, they must.

In a similar vein, the CEO is the person who lifts those around them. Are your team members engaged in tasks that are the best use of their time? If not, then how can you get them to that place?

The way to do this is to automate what you can and develop consistent, reliable processes that will give you and your team the support you need to excel.

Automation

We could not run Connecticut Trial Firm without relying heavily on technology. If we used paper files, we would require larger offices with more room for filing cabinets. If we did not use a digital filing system, we would not have the flexibility to work remotely and cover for each other. Firm operations would have ground to a halt if we'd spread Covid in the office back in 2020 rather than working from home for twelve months. Tech doesn't just make us better; in many ways, it defines who we are.

We have a policy of automating everything we can. If a computer can complete a task, it should, because that frees humans to do higher-level tasks. When I was a baby attorney working for a large firm, I would pore through our firm database in search of models for complaints, interrogatories—you name it. What a waste. Today we've created templates in Filevine that will automatically pull case details into a document, saving us time and improving accuracy.

Maybe you're not drafting complaints, and that's great. But if your team is unnecessarily bogged down by detail work, that leaves them with less time to tap into their own unique talents. As CEO, think about the tasks you can automate. Do you need someone to schedule calls with clients, or can the clients do it themselves through a service like Acuity? Can bills be set to auto-pay? You get the idea.

Automate what you can. It will result in a lot of time saved.

Hiring

We have been conservative with our hiring. When we hired our first paralegal, we did math on a napkin at Panera and hoped for the best. Years later, each hire still requires a deep breath and a psychological adjustment. But when you're severely understaffed, it requires something else: speed.

We staff our team with a number of virtual assistants who live internationally. They are as much a part of our team as anyone else, and we use a service called Get Staffed Up to vet candidates for us instead of searching on our own. Our international team members are phenomenal. They act as legal assistants and receptionists and they help us to communicate with Spanish-speaking clients. When we need a team member in a hurry, we have gone this route. You can also use head hunters or staffing agencies if you need someone in physical proximity. The idea is to outsource the hiring process to someone who understands your needs and will present you with the best candidates.

Operating Systems

If you brought on a new team member tomorrow to assist you, would they know how to perform their job duties? No, let me rephrase: could they refer to a written manual to learn how to perform their job duties, or would you have to answer all the little questions that inevitably arise?

No matter how obvious a task may seem to you, it's not. Your team needs documented systems. How is mail handled? What do people say when answering the phone? If a potential new client asks for a referral, is there a list available? I'll bet that you have opinions about how certain job duties should be handled, but if a system isn't documented, it doesn't exist. This will lead employees to either guess, spend time worrying about their lack of knowledge, or interrupt you—possibly all three.

We have both videos and written instructions for our systems, and our newest team members rave about them. They don't want to bother anyone, but they also want to succeed at their job. Documented systems give them what they need.

As leaders, we also rely on these systems because they serve as institutional memory. Every time we confront a new situation—whether it's about holidays, or paid leave, or overtime—we spend time as a leadership team deciding what our policy will be. Then we memorialize the policy. This ensures that we apply rules fairly and that we don't time on the same problem more than once.

As you grow, you can get your team on board and develop a culture of sharing knowledge by writing down job duties, passwords, contacts—anything! We have pages for team allergies and favorite lunch orders in case we're ordering and someone is in a meeting. Information should not exist exclusively in anyone's head. This is not only great for onboarding but minimizes damage to the business if someone leaves.

Your team members may not see the value in this at first. We used to have firm goals to create fifty Tettra pages a quarter just to get this project started. But I don't think anyone on our team would argue against Tettra today. Creating pages is second nature. This is our operating manual, and it is one of our firm's most precious resources.

Ryan McKeen

If you are going to become a law firm CEO, you will need a lot of tools. You will need things like computers, notebooks, and phones. You will also need a person or people whose job it is to acquire, organize, and inventory those tools. This chapter from me will focus on none of those things. It will focus on the most important tools you will need—your skills.

Hiring

When we started hiring, we hired friends, friends of friends, and whoever we could find on a job website. It sometimes worked but often didn't.

Over time, we strengthened our hiring process. We built systems to deliver us high-quality applicants and developed an ability to vet those applicants to determine whether they were going to add to our team or detract from it.

One of the very best things that we did was to engage a hiring consultant to help us through these decisions. The consultant does testing and then explains the test results to us if we need explanations.

The job of CEO is in part to assemble the team to deliver results. That means your organization must always be hiring. And in order to obtain the talent you need, a key piece of your job is going to be recruiting.

The people you will need to grow and scale your firm are likely happily employed and have many options. It will be your job to convince these people that your firm is their best option. Recruiting people better than you at jobs is the only way forward.

Coaches, Mentors, and Therapists

This could be in the "The People You Will Need" chapter, but I'm putting it here. You are the ultimate tool that both you and your organization need.

Every single CEO that I know who has achieved a high level of success has a coach or even multiple coaches.

The reason for this is simple. If you are truly a CEO of your law firm, you have few peers. Very few people have founded and grown any business of any size. To do it at scale is statistically very rare. There are a lot of people who can help you start a firm or even grow it into seven figures in annual gross revenue.

When you climb higher than that, the air gets much thinner. The decisions become much more complicated. And the number of people you can turn to for good advice and guidance becomes increasingly small.

Coaches who have worked with successful CEOs or have been one themselves are a great resource. They understand the pressures and complexities of you face. And they have seen success and failure many times over. They can help you see the way forward where others can't. Having a coach can accelerate your growth many times over—and in the process, make you a lot more money.

Mentors are also incredibly valuable. I distinguish them from coaches because the relationship is often less formal. They are people who will take your call and share their thoughts on a problem. If you are going to succeed, you will need about a dozen of these people in your contacts.

You will also need to do work on yourself. Many of the problems your organization will face are caused by problems between your ears. Firms are in many ways shadows of their founders and leaders.

Understanding what you are good at and what you are not is invaluable, as is understanding what motivates you and why and what deeply held beliefs are holding you back.

In my case, for years, I didn't hire anyone. I grew up middle-class, and the lesson I learned was that a dollar spent was one less dollar that I had. I had internalized this belief. When you run a business, it takes money to make money, and some of the highest returns on earth come from investing in your team and firm. It took therapy for me to work through this.

Money

Growth eats cash. There is no way around this. Whether you obtain a home equity line of credit, borrow against your retirement, get a line of credit, or work for years at under market rate—you will need more money. Money is the tool of tools that you will use to mold the world to the vision of your firm.

One of the best things we did was to use a company to fund our case expenses. It enabled us to use money we were dumping into cases on things like hiring, marketing, and technology. It also gave us access to the best experts in the world as we could pay them.

There are no easy solutions here, but spend time making, understanding, and growing your money.

Technology and Data

These two things go hand in hand. The best technology will give you the best data. It will collect data in the background and show it to you in ways that are useful.

The smartest firm owners I know view technology expenses as an investment and not a liability on the balance sheet.

You should determine whatever the best-in-class software is for what you do and pay the price the vendor is asking.

You should also buy software that can scale with you.

We invested in leads management software (a CRM) when we were getting ten leads a month. Why did we do this? We did it because converting those ten leads was incredibly important for our firm.

We also did it to start building systems and processes for a future with more leads. The result is that as we have experienced a significant increase in demand for our services, we have been able to easily meet that demand because we had perfected our intake systems. Making it rain is only part of the equation—catching the rain is every bit as important.

Now we have years' worth of intake data that leads to better decisions surrounding marketing and staffing.

Software doesn't require a salary, and it doesn't take a break. It is only going to get better. You should make deep investments in technology if you want to thrive.

Michelle Dellino

The most important "tools" are your systems. You need the systems in place to carry out the functions in your firm. After you have the systems, you also need the software to implement the systems. The systems come first, the software comes second, and having someone in the right seat to implement it all is critical. As CEO, you cannot be the one using all the tools to make things work. However, you will need to help build the systems and select the tools.

You need a "tech stack." This is the stack of software tools you will get the most out of, learn to utilize, and roll out to your team. Evaluating your tech stack at least once a year is a good idea. We have practice management software, intake/sales software, financial software, voice over IP phone system software, internal communication via Slack, and a handful of other pieces in our tech stack. You should figure out what software you need for your systems, use your leadership or technology team to evaluate what works best for what you need, and stick with it. Regular evaluation of the tools for cost and what works best is important, but changing things too often will likely make you less efficient and frustrate your team. You should beware of "shiny object syndrome." I have suffered from this many times, always wanting to grab on to the next new piece of software or new tool or trying something out with the team just because other people were. Once I stopped doing this and established a schedule and system for reevaluating current and new tools, both hardware and software, my team was better for it.

I also want to talk about a tool that you may not think of in your role as CEO of the firm. These are your mental and physical health tools. Let's call them "wellness tools." You are only going to be as good in this role as your own mental health and physical health allow you to be. I spent the first several years of my firm neglecting my mental and physical health and focusing on one thing: driving business. This made me successful financially and drove some amazing growth but took a major toll on my overall wellness. When I started to think about what tools I needed to get these areas under control, my life got better. I lost the nearly seventy pounds I gained while I built my firm plus some more. I went from never working out and eating horribly to working out most days and feeling in control of what fuels my body—all while I was busier than ever. I never could have done this without establishing wellness tools to help me and actually using them.

You will want to think about what works for you and how to implement a schedule that utilizes wellness tools. This needs to be a deliberate choice and it needs to be actionable. On the physical side, determine what you need to stay healthy and fit. Do you need to go to the gym? Are you someone who will never set foot in a gym and needs to have something to use at home? Will you walk for your cardio, or do you want to ride your bike? This looks different for everyone, but you do need a fitness plan and the tools in place to carry it out. How will you manage your diet, and what does healthy eating look like for you? If you love to cook, you can plan for that. If you know you will never cook and don't turn on the oven, you need tools and a plan to avoid the traps of convenience eating.

You also cannot neglect your mental health. What do you need to mentally disconnect from your firm so you can refresh your mind and be present when you spend time with your family? How do you manage the stress that comes with the CEO role and law firm culture in general? Whatever those things are, identify them, make some part of your schedule, and stick to it.

No one ever has time to go to therapy, work out, or meal plan. You have to make the time. I always said I did not have time until I realized I could not afford to keep neglecting to make time.

You also won't always have the motivation to exercise or eat well. Relying on motivation will get you nowhere. Just like you won't be able to run your firm or build your firm simply by being motivated, you will not be able to stay physically fit and stick to a healthy eating plan and exercise program relying on motivation alone. No one is motivated 100 percent of the time. You will need to utilize discipline. Discipline builds strong people and teams. You will need to work out when you don't want to and pass on the dessert when you want it. You will need to find a therapist, even if you don't want to, so you have that resource when you need it. Having these kinds of tools in place is one thing. You can have a Peloton, full home gym, personal chef, and therapist on speed dial, but you will need discipline to make it work and use the tools. Discipline and diligence win the day every time over inspiration and motivation. You owe it to yourself, your family, and your team to be healthy and strong.

Your team might also need help finding the right mental and physical health tools. One-on-ones at our firm include checking in with people on their mental and physical health. When we had an attorney who was really struggling to get exercise in at the gym, we problem-solved and made the arrangement to get him a Peloton at home to use. I'm not saying you need to buy everyone on your team a Peloton, but think outside of the box about the tools they need. We provide a cash stipend every month for people to spend on wellness. Providing your team with the tools for health and wellness and the time to use it goes a long way to building and maintaining a healthy team.

CHAPTER 5

The Vision Forward

Bill Umansky

I have been fortunate to run a great seven-figure practice for the past several years and hope to meet our goal of an eight-figure law firm very soon. If you read the original *Tiger Tactics*, you know that more than I wanted money, I wanted to work with great fearless people who are leaders in the community and hard-chargers in the court room who give back to the community they came from. My vision hasn't changed much in the past twenty-plus years. I haven't really thought about the vision forward until recently. Recent health issues, including enduring more than eight surgeries, have made me really zero in on what the future holds. Over the past couple years and in advance of writing my chapters for this book, I started thinking about the next steps for my life and the law firm.

I have made some money, but know I do not have enough to retire and live in the fashion I currently desire. Perhaps I made some financial mistakes I hope you don't make, and at fifty-six years old, I know I must grind it out for another ten years or so. Right now, I want to continue to build and work with high-quality people who want to work with me doing something special in Orlando and Central Florida. Over the next few years, I will start turning over more and more leadership of the law firm to some younger lawyers who care about clients and our community as much as I do.

I am can see myself still being involved in my firm until I am in my late sixties. However, my role is changing. I want to be a full-time business coach by sixty-two years old. I still want to rain-make for my law firm, but I understand that as I transition to coaching it will be harder to do that, so I must hire and coach my lawyers to be better and better rain makers. I want to continue to mold and teach my leadership team and the lawyers I believe will run our law firm. I see my firm potentially changing names but having systems in place that outlast my own legacy. Hopefully those systems will continue to evolve as software, technology, and cool things like artificial intelligence are always evolving. I look forward to watching other lawyers take operations and systems we put in place to a new level. I want my leadership team to take what they have learned and be able to coach other law firm owners on the things we did right and did wrong so these young owners can build something special in their own communities. I realize that I may make less profit from my law firm, as I am relying upon others to run the business, but I will make up the income through my coaching business. My vision moving forward is to pass as much knowledge and wisdom along with care to the new generation of young law firm owners who will face new challenges in their practices. My hope is that I can create a generation of future mentors. The practice of law truly is a privilege, and it is incumbent upon successful lawyers to pass the experience and knowledge they have acquired to the next generations of lawyers.

Billie Tarascio

The Future of Law

Law firms will look different in twenty years. They will face consolidation. Old-school business models will not be able to keep up with the nimble, tech-enabled and deregulated firms around them. That will also mean volatility. We saw this volatility emerge from the pandemic, and I do not think we will see that slow down.

Arizona has deregulated. The prohibition on fee splitting is gone. Not only do we have a fully functioning and formal referral program, but we are also bringing on non-attorney salespeople who will be compensated based 100 percent on commission. Soon, Modern Law will have a sales team utilizing the best practices in sales.

Another massive change is allowing LPs to practice law. The monopoly on the practice of law is disappearing. For owners, this means a larger availability of practitioners to hire and generate revenue on your behalf (and less of the ego that comes from lawyers).

A third very important change is allowing non-lawyer ownership. This means outside money, and it means consolidation. Will you be swallowing other firms, or will you be swallowed? We are swallowing. Just this week, we are hiring two solo practitioners because they can make as much money as they were previously and have the support of a progressive law firm behind them while they work from home with autonomy and flexibility. New law looks very good to sole practitioners.

Hopefully one day, at the height of consolidation, we will be ready to be bought out for a large amount of money. Law firms will become more valuable as deregulation spreads.

The Future for Modern Law

In the next ten years, we will have fifty practitioners (attorneys and LPs) and be all over the state of Arizona. Our brand will be stronger, and we will have increased our market share. Sole practitioners will love the ability to work remote and have a supportive back-office law firm handling their marketing, collections, training, and more. The firm will have a CFO and CMO, and I may or may not still be the CEO.

By continuing to invest in branding, marketing, and sales, we will pay very well and attract top talent. Attorneys can specialize in anything they want to specialize in. There is ample business in our growing market in Phoenix. We must invest in management, in leadership, and in a sustainable culture. We must be protective of our firm, keeping out terroristic diva attorneys, slackers, or downers who pollute the culture of growth, expansion, and hope.

The Future for Billie Tarascio

I will continue to buy commercial office space leased by Modern Law and have rental income as a stream of income apart from legal services. I will continue to invest in online course offerings related to the things I know well: divorce and family law firm operations and family law litigation. These are two separate markets where specialized knowledge can be packaged and sold. The online course market and online communities concept is still expanding and evolving. I really hope to evolve in my role at Modern Law and hire people better equipped than I am to run the firm.

Advice for You

You will see the world, your future, and the future of law differently than I do. Your firm vision should be one that you are confident about and one that resonates with you. There are many ways to build something beautiful and special—but with all the challenges in business, if you are not staying true to yourself, you will lose your way. There will be moments of doubt. Weekends plagued by fear and anxiety when things go wrong. They will go wrong. All you can do is learn and recover as quickly as possible, but never doubt your core beliefs.

I hope this book helps you know that you are not alone. Some ideas will resonate. Some concepts will not work at all. The future of law is rapidly changing, with new technologies and deregulation disrupting traditional business models. As a result, law firms must be nimble, tech-enabled, and innovative to survive and thrive in this new landscape.

At Modern Law, we are embracing these changes and investing in branding, marketing, and sales to differentiate ourselves from the competition and attract new clients. We are also expanding our team to include LPs and non-attorney salespeople and investing in leadership and culture to build a sustainable and successful firm.

My advice to others is to stay true to your core beliefs and vision, even in the face of challenges and setbacks. The future of law may be uncertain, but by focusing on innovation, leadership, and a strong brand, we can create something beautiful and special that will endure for years to come.

Allison McKeen

The practice of law has changed tremendously since I passed the bar not even twenty years ago, but the fear surrounding those changes has been constant. When my first employer gave us cell phones, colleagues worried that they would be on call twenty-four hours a day. What would it mean when those cell phones were able to check email? Would the partners expect responses at midnight? Would clients? It took me months to convince one of my employers that we should be able to work from home outside of business hours rather than trekking into the office. "But how will we know you're working?" they demanded. "Why would you hire people you don't trust?" I thought.

When Ryan opened a paperless law firm, other lawyers clutched their pearls. They claimed it was unethical to use cloud storage, or to use Gmail for business, or to blog about anything having to do with the practice of law. ("Readers will think you're their lawyer!")

And you know what happened? None of their fears for our paperless firm materialized. We embraced technology and became more efficient, more responsive, and more organized than the old guard. The youngest members of our team don't bat an eye when we say we're paperless. They haven't worked any other way.

That's not where we stopped. For our 100-million-dollar verdict, we used animation to reconstruct an accident and injuries for the jury while the defense used PowerPoint slides. We pulled excerpts of deposition transcripts onto a screen instantly to impeach witnesses while the defense read from paper. Basically, what we did was to anticipate what the jury expected to see, and we would have been at a disadvantage if we hadn't met their expectations.

The biggest problems for personal injury cases can be found in the details. In the future, we will use AI to organize massive amounts of medical records in seconds, finding those proverbial needles in the haystack. We expect defense firms will do the same.

My point is that technology is here and artificial intelligence is poised to play a major role in the future of law. There's no sense fighting it. You can choose to see tech as a threat or as an opportunity, and I see it as the latter. Rather than being chained to our laptops and cell phones, our team sets boundaries with our clients and with each other so everyone knows not to expect a response outside of business hours. Our firm instituted a "right to disconnect" policy that states it's okay to turn off Slack and ignore email when you need to focus on something. Instead of ruining our personal lives, technology makes it possible for us to be home with our loved ones when they are sick, or to skip the commute and squeeze in an extra hour of work so we have time to attend the school assembly. It's given us the chance to be complete humans.

And this is where the opportunity lies: how do you use technology to be more human? The days of writing briefs and engaging in detail work are numbered, but I believe that human connection will remain a quiet, desperate need. How will we remain engaged and connected in a time when technology makes it so easy to text rather than call?

The future of our firm's practice is in more community outreach. Technology has allowed us to think about long-term goals that involve service, not money. If we gain an extra hour a day because of technological advances, can we use that time to volunteer? If we're no longer preparing medical chronologies and writing briefs, can we spend more time comforting our clients? In short, we look at ways to harness technology to create a better world for ourselves and others.

We have the chance to do a lot of good and bring healing if we accept the changes coming. You're the visionary and the architect of your firm, so how will you adapt your practice in this time of rapid change? What does your team need from you, their leader?

Above all, don't listen to the afraid. The future of our profession is bright when we choose to see it that way.

Sandy Van

A strong vision is needed to run a successful business. Without a strong vision, your business will fall prey to bad employees and inefficient processes. That is why my vision is crystal clear: hire the best people, get rid of the dead weight, and turn my firm into one of the largest, most recognizable law firms there is. This vision is lofty but doable, just like yours might be. You have to challenge yourself and step outside your comfort zone in order to grow. It is not going to be easy. But learning from my story may help you evade, face, and overcome challenges or obstacles that come your way.

The vision for my firm is enormous, and the only way to achieve the desired results is to be an efficient, lean, mean, killing law firm machine. We need to make sure the firm is running efficiently with great team members, processes, and use of technology. To achieve this vision, I plan on learning every day. Whether it is from books, conferences, podcasts, or my fellow brilliant business and legal minds, learning is key to my personal journey. This includes learning about areas unrelated to law and personal injury.

I think you can ultimately learn anything that you put your mind to, whether it is a new area of law or a new skill set—watch

YouTube videos, read books, attend conferences, or purchase courses. All problems have solutions that can be found with effort and determination. I love starting new projects, and the skills that I learn from those projects can complement other businesses of mine. The best advice is often found in the most unusual places, and that is where I would be looking. From tech gurus to self-made billionaires, the best way to achieve success is to learn from others' mistakes and from each other. My firm focuses on personal injury cases right now, but I want to expand into related areas. To do that, I need the right people. It's important to let go of employees who are not committed to the firm's vision. The reality is that tough decisions must be made for the good of the company, and salaries should reflect results. Hiring above-average people who align with the firm's vision increases productivity and benefits clients. The success and growth of your company depends heavily on hiring the right people.

Next, I want to simplify complicated processes because I'm also planning to expand my firm's services to other states. This move requires careful planning and strategic decision-making. To ensure that the expansion is successful, the company as a whole will need to research the laws and market conditions in each state. I believe that the expertise and experience in my firm's current practice areas can benefit clients in other regions, and I'm excited about the prospect of reaching a wider audience. Although expanding into new areas isn't easy, my team and I are committed to taking the necessary steps to ensure that our expansion is well-planned and executed so our clients continue to receive the highest level of service and support.

Mario Godoy

Defining and clarifying the vision of your firm is one of the most important things you can do as an owner. The vision is what inspires your staff and clients to work with your firm.

I actively practice planning ahead—every day, every week, every month, every year—and charting out where the firm will be two years or five years from now and how it will get there. I do the same planning for myself, personally: what my personal goals, career goals, financial goals, family goals—and what I have to do to achieve those goals.

Vision forward is seeing myself, my law firm, my clients, and my team where they want to be in the future—not just today.

It's not only about me and my goals—it's where the firms, my partner, and my team members want to be.

As an immigrant, I started Godoy Law to help other immigrants achieve their American Dream and not experience some of the hurtful, devastating things that happened to my own family when they got bad legal advice.

Part of my vision forward was to start an estate planning law firm, because I saw what happened to my grandmother and I wanted to help other people protect the future of their loved ones. Even though I didn't have any estate planning legal expertise, I started Estate and Probate Legal Group with my partner Steven Novak, a great estate planning attorney. Steve leads the legal department at EPLG. I took all of the lessons—and mistakes—that I learned from starting and growing Godoy and converted those to a brand-new firm that is incorporated separately and as its own separate entity.

And I always like to tell folks, "Don't make the mistakes I did." I hit every entrepreneurial mistake on the "don't do that" list.

EPLG Vision

For Estate and Probate Legal Group, my vision forward is to make an impact on the people who work there—to grow something that will reach all of their goals, including those of my partner, Steve. I know that in helping that team reach its potential, we will save families from destroying themselves through the probate process.

Some people like collecting baseball cards—but when I'm not working on Godoy, I like working on EPLG. I enjoy helping people during a transitionary period in their life, whether it's personal or professional. I never practiced this type of law; I never delivered those legal services as an attorney. I am in the leadership role. I have the vision and experience to build something great, a working machine to bring in other great lawyers who want to be practitioners but don't want to manage a law firm. My vision is for EPLG to grow and help people practice law and to help their clients. Because I have a partnership with Steve, it's very different from Godoy, where I'm the sole owner. EPLG has grown every year, and it's meeting its goals—both the firm goals and the people goals.

Mario-ism:

Create your own ladder.

At Godoy, I'm the owner as well as holding the management leadership role. Godoy is going to be my life's work, something that will outlive me. It's my personal mission as an immigrant myself.

The opportunities in this country are enormous. People come here because there is something they can't get in their home country, but immigrants need to be able to work for it; the *pursuit* of happiness is guaranteed, not happiness itself. Immigrants who have the inner drive to pursue what they want can come and make a better future, and that's what I'm building—a conduit to help build for others what my family and I built for ourselves.

Immigrants are the engine of our economy, and I want to facilitate that. So many businesses are founded by immigrants or first-generation Americans. Scientific breakthroughs, technology... in *Scaling Up: How a Few Companies Make It...and Why the Rest Don't*

by Verne Harnish, the dedication reads:

To the leaders who scale up... you are the engines of our economies.

I did not have a hand up or someone who would give me a position in a good law firm when I passed the bar exam, so I created my own ladder. My business then turned around and employed more people, many of them with an immigration story, and together we contribute to building America. I am scaling up and teaching other lawyers how to scale up too.

We are all better by having immigrants, and the continued renewal of ideas. What we're building at Godoy Law will perpetually give opportunity to immigrants who want to pursue success and happiness.

My big audacious dream, my vision forward, is that my grandkids will see and respect what I have built. What I am continuing to build.

Michelle Dellino

In the CEO role, you are the visionary for your firm. Your vision will extend to the team you lead if you are doing this role well. The vision forward for you, your team, and the profession is anything but the same for every one of us.

For My Firm

We spend a few days away together as a firm on a retreat every year. We didn't always do this, but now that we have started, we will never stop doing it. This time allows us to look at where we are and where we are going. I believe to embrace the vision, your team needs to know and understand what it is on a base level. Even if, in the beginning as CEO, you can only take the team away for a day, I encourage you to take time away from the office in this manner, share your vision, and bring your team together.

My team at DFLG has growth and execution plans in the short term and long term. We have core values to guide our team and its plans and to keep our vision on course. My vision this year is more focused than ever on the health of my team. I love the team I have in a way that I never have before. There have been many incarnations of the DFLG team over the past decade. There will be many of your team, too. Finally, we have a team that is highly supportive, lacks drama or toxicity, and is committed to each other and our clients. This sounds easier to build than it really is. It has taken time, many mistakes, and a lot of ups and downs to have such a strong team. Now that we have them, I am taking my support of them and the firm's support of them to the next level with everything we are doing. I want to be the best leader I can be for this team and provide them with all the best things to live their best lives and thrive both in the profession and in their lives.

For You

This is an exciting time to lead a law firm. The practice of law is as fluid as it has ever been with so much legal tech and outside-the-box structures that include hybrid and work from home options like never before. You have the chance to do whatever you want from the CEO leadership seat of your firm and to create the firm you want, so it is important to remember how powerful that truly is. Your vision and your actions to implement it will shape so much for the people who work for you and their families, your clients, and even your clients' families. You should dream big, but do not neglect the planning aspect of implementing the dream. You have a responsibility to your team to take care of them and lead with purpose, not in chaos. Everyone has worked at that place that was an operational disaster with toxic people, constant starting over, and no consistency. Do not be that place or that person. Implement your vision with purpose. You do not have to do it all at once—and you probably can't—so be strategic with what big things you want to do in a given quarter and year.

I am the kind of person who always has to be working on the next thing. I have a ton of big ideas. I become obsessed with doing one thing but then also changing something else. You probably are too if you are in the CEO seat of your firm. Something that anchors me in being this kind of a person is my personal understanding and practice of "hold on tightly, let go lightly." This is a notion that focuses on the yin and yang balance between two ideas and simultaneous actions. It is about a balance between two ideas that are largely juxtaposed to one another. The first is being fully committed and going all in, and the second is the flexibility to adapt and make changes when needed. The balanced idea of "hold on tightly, let go lightly" is the very heart what I consider a successful life and firm. Recently, I had to say goodbye to the longest tenured team member at my firm. For years, I had held on tightly through the good and bad as a part of staying loyal and true to this person and our roots on the team. Finally, the time came to let go lightly and adapt to the necessary change for the betterment of the firm and this person. As you think about your vision and its implementation, you will gravitate to the need to hold on tightly. You will want security and safety for your firm and yourself. Nonetheless, never forget that you have to always be ready to let go lightly as part of necessary growth and change.

In many ways, the CEO seat is a never-ending job. You will probably never be on vacation and not think about your team. You might always have that next big idea and be working on how to execute, jotting down thoughts or dictating on your phone's notes application while at Sunday brunch. Your work is never really done. You can always be better, and so can your team. It is exhausting yet exhilarating. Everything is always your problem when the chips are down. But this CEO role is the greatest privilege and seat of all in the professional realm for those of us with this calling. With all the pressure and responsibility also comes a great deal of freedom. Once you start to execute and dial in the people, systems, and leadership skills, you will have the freedom to do and be anything you want. Stay true to your vision and always hold on tightly, let go lightly.

If you ever want to talk about your journey, please reach out to me. I wish you all the best as you move forward as CEO.

Jenn Gore-Cuthbert

Why Grow, Grow, Grow?

People often ask me why I am so determined to grow my law firm so fast. The reason is simple—every time I encountered a problem, I had to find a way to solve it, and growth was mainly the solution. Also, I firmly believe that the problems I face today are much better than the ones I dealt with when my firm was much smaller.

I have learned that having only one person in a department can be extremely risky for any business. If that person falls ill, takes time off, or leaves the company, the entire department can grind to a halt. Over the years, I have had to step in and take control of departments that were left unstaffed due to staff absences or departures.

Therefore, I have made it a priority to grow my law firm quickly by bringing in more staff to each department. This not only ensures that each department has more than one person working in it but also allows for more efficient delegation of tasks and a higher level of expertise across the board. Ultimately, this has enabled my firm to handle larger and more complex cases, and it has contributed significantly to our success. This makes the firm much more sustainable.

Working with Professionals

Expanding our firm has provided us with more leverage, including the opportunity to collaborate with highly skilled and experienced professionals. I am excited about the prospect of working with even more talented individuals in the future. I remember when our firm was smaller and it was difficult to attract top talent. We didn't have the same brand recognition and perks to offer as larger firms. But now, as we continue to grow, we're starting to draw people in like a magnet. It's amazing how much easier it is to communicate our vision and purpose as a larger firm, and it's been so rewarding to see that reflected in the caliber of people who want to work with us.

Our firm has come a long way, and it's exciting to think about how much further we can go. We've established ourselves as a reputable and desirable workplace, and I'm confident that our growth will continue to bring us top talent that will help us achieve even greater success.

Developing a law firm that not only creates great value in the world but also helps many people is a highly rewarding experience. As I approach my tenth year in business, I find it increasingly fulfilling to impact the lives of not only the clients we serve but also our team members. Seeing our staff grow, be professionally coached, learn, develop and thrive is highly rewarding. I love seeing people step into their full potential and leverage their talents.

Mentoring and Giving Back

Mentoring and coaching newer CEOs and lawyers has been an incredibly gratifying experience for me. Witnessing someone with the same drive and passion I possess, and who is willing to put in the work to achieve their desired results, is truly exciting! Sometimes it's easy to forget all the knowledge you've acquired is completely foreign to someone further behind you on their journey.

The Future of Law

Undoubtedly, the law firms of the future will be more automated and efficient, with better systems and data. I believe in my heart that the primary role of a lawyer or law firm is to advocate for others. And no matter what happens, I believe people will still need people to advocate for them. We live in a world full of information, but no one knows how to use or leverage it. People don't know which way to go, left or right.

The legal landscape is constantly evolving, and to stay relevant, we all must embrace new technologies and systems. The ability to collect and analyze data, automate legal documents, and streamline the legal process will significantly transform the industry and exponentially expand our ability to create. I believe that it is imperative to adopt this mindset now to prepare to thrive in the coming years. Those who resist this change risk being left behind by the competition.

For far too long, the legal industry has been complacent and inefficient. We must continue to embrace technology and find innovative ways to make advocating for others a more effective experience. By prioritizing these areas, we can achieve great legal outcomes that make a real difference in our clients' lives. At the end of the day, our goal should be to create a legal industry that is more efficient, effective, and client-centric.

My Future Vision

One thing I've come to realize is that no matter how much I think I know now, in a few years, I'll probably look back and realize how little I knew. That's why I believe it's crucial to stay in a perpetual state of growth and change. We must be open to the ways our vision will change, as opportunities beyond our wildest dreams can come unexpectedly at a moment's notice. The only true security you will ever have is your ability and willingness to adapt and change to whatever you come up against.

As we continue to learn and grow, our perspectives will evolve, and our vision will grow and change. Embrace the journey and the unexpected twists and turns along the way. Be willing to adapt and pivot when necessary and keep pushing forward. Who knows what amazing experiences and opportunities lie just around the corner?

Allison Williams

Once upon a time, I lived for the courtroom. My practice area necessitated my mastering the art of trying cases with little to no discovery on a moment's notice. Leaving the courtroom to build a business was one of the greatest internal struggles I ever overcame; however, I realized early on that I could not create more of the outcomes I desired in the world for the people I desire to help unless I devoted my attention to building a business that would 10X my outcomes.

The journey to becoming a law firm owner was fraught with struggle, challenge, and trauma. Much of what I knew—or thought I knew—about myself, my desires, my goals and aspirations was faulty. I had strengths I never knew existed. I had weaknesses I thought I had long ago overcome. I learned how much more capable I was than I ever believed. And I began to give myself permission to be less than perfect, while simultaneously being more than enough.

Not a journey for the faint at heart—which is the journey to becoming a law firm CEO is sooooo much more than the tips and tricks lawyers download from the internet.

Once I started to create consistency, reliability, predictability, and great outcomes in business, I fell in love with the "high" of being good in business. From there, as a natural helper, I desired to create more lawyers who are also "good in business." I realized that my unique blend of strategic thinking and systematic approaches, when paired with my deeply empathic nature, could achieve not only my desired outcome of more lawyers who are "good in business" but also lawyers who actually enjoyed the process of creating. Hence, my second company, Law Firm Mentor (LFM), was born.

I now run two successful multiple seven-figure companies—my law firm and my law firm coaching company. My dreams, however, are in their infancy. As is inherent in human nature, creating more in life opens one's awareness to (quite shockingly!) even more in life. I have several plans for my future, but the one universal gift I want to give to all of you is that you continually seek to create more for your future. "More" does not mean simply building bigger because you can, but genuinely tapping into what satisfies the soul and brings more of your true self into being. That only happens through creating abundant resources so that you can exponentially increase your reach in whatever area of life suits you.

For me, I have a passion for helping families in familial distress. Williams Law Group will continue to be a leader in matrimonial law, family law, and child abuse and neglect law. The firm has recently acquired another law firm and added criminal defense to our roster of services. I have also reignited my passion to grow the firm, and we are in the process of expanding our reach into other areas. My goal is to create a place where families can receive the highest quality of legal representation to strengthen their ties as a family—be that through legacy planning, elder care and advocacy, real estate investment, acquisition, and disposition, or a host of other related services. The world is my oyster!

As a member of the legal profession, my heart will always be with lawyers. My desire is to continue to help lawyers to become good in business and to create more of their desired outcomes in the world through the vehicle of their law firm businesses. To that end, LFM is only a few years old but is already serving hundreds of lawyers. My desire is to continue to scale LFM, providing services to law firm owners, administrative professionals, and team members and those who assist them.

Most critically, I desire to continue to create. At my core, I am a creative and a builder. I am not satisfied in life if I am not building something... strategies, plans, businesses, empires. I have learned that about myself through working with a variety of intellectual and intuitive professionals. For all of you, I desire that you find the true essence of yourself and tap into exponential ecstasy by bringing more of yourself into the world. A law firm is a beautiful yet complex and intricate ecosystem. By employing the strategies outlined in this book, you have approached the starting point of mastering your ecosystem, which is the beginning of so much more that lies ahead on the journey called life. The world is your oyster—so long as you remember to crush chaos in business and to never stop growing.

Joey Vitale

Vision. Mission. Purpose. These are big words. Most business owners don't take the time to reflect on them. And those who do often walk away overwhelmed and without any clear answers.

So let's just cut to the chase and talk about success. Because I want success for you, and I'm sure you want success for yourself. But what is success?

Success is simply getting what you want.

The problem, of course, is that most people don't know what they want. If someone doesn't know what they want, they borrow other people's dreams and goals. What you want should be an honest and accurate answer, not what others will see as success.

So, what do you really want?

Let me pause here. I understand that this simple question might feel incredibly difficult to answer. But it's critical to reflect on it and find an answer that lights you up. Otherwise, success will always feel out of reach for you because you never made it clear enough to know when you achieved it.

In this chapter, I'd like to share with you how I've defined success for myself—what I've decided I really want. I share this not because I think that your definition of success should match mine. I share because I am on my own journey of figuring out what I truly want. It's my hope that, by reading my conclusions, you can more confidently and boldly declare what it is you truly want for yourself.

I want to design myself entirely out of the legal and client work at my law firm. As my law firm grows, I realize my time is more valuable outside of client work. To be blunt, I also just enjoy the other parts of running the firm more. I have worked my way to only spending an hour or less a week on client work, and I want to continue building my team and processes so that this part of the firm can run completely without me.

I want a law firm that can thrive, and not just survive, without me. It's no accident that my law firm, Indie Law, doesn't have my name attached to it. While I have no plans to sell it in the near future, I want it to be as valuable an asset as possible in the future. It's one thing to have your firm survive while you take extended time off. It's quite another for the firm to continue attracting and converting prospective clients in your absence. I am slowly transitioning myself out of our branding and marketing so that the firm's growth is not as dependent on me.

I want to participate in long-term sustainability efforts. I believe that people today have an obligation to consider our actions so that future generations are more likely to thrive. Environmental trends will never go away, and I believe it's important for my law firm to be a leader in sustainability. That's why we have committed to planting twenty trees for every trademark package we sell. We have a big goal to plant one million trees by 2032.

I want to give my wife the option to retire or work less. As I learned about business owners "retiring" their partners, I initially wanted to do the same. But my wife is an absolute rock star at her job and has no desire to stop working any time soon. And so what I really want is not to retire her, but to give her the option to do so if and when she pleases.

I want to surround myself with people who have epic abundance. While I am committed to being a servant leader, to giving back to the community, and to cheering on my colleagues—I am also very protective of my inner circle. Scarcity mindsets are sneaky, and there are very few people I trust to consistently maintain a mindset of "epic abundance" around me. Those with epic abundance put community over competition, facts over feelings, possibilities over problems, and curiosity over control. For the sake of my business—our clients, our team, and our mission—I am very intentional about spending as much time as possible with the most abundant people in my network.

I want to get out of Chicago every February and travel somewhere where I can wear shorts. I'll be very straight with you. I'm not very money motivated. I value flexibility and freedom. My wife and I don't have children beyond our dog and cat. My wife works remotely and travels for her job. We don't have very expensive tastes, but we value experiences together—especially if they rescue us from the Chicago winter. (I love Chicago, but my

Sicilian genes can only tolerate freezing weather for so long!) The more money I make, the more consistently we can have family getaway vacations when it gets cold.

I want to make a bigger impact beyond my law firm. The more I grow my business, the more passionate I get about helping others do the same. And while I love my law firm's mission to be the best brand protectors we can be, I feel called to help more business owners play offense, not just defense. Through my own journey, I've discovered that building a powerful team you can trust is the ultimate business growth advantage. That is why I have created a separate business, Skybreaker™, which helps entrepreneurs create strong teams so they can become more profitable, stress-free, and liberated CEOs. Clarifying this vision has been a big challenge for me, but I'm realizing that I just want to see what I'm capable of and make the biggest impact I can with the time I have.

Elise Buie

Vision forward—So what's next? Well, that is a complicated question that I have been pondering over the last six months or so. Last year was an extremely challenging year for me both personally and professionally. My pregnant bookkeeper, who was also my first PNW friend, was suddenly and tragically killed in a seaplane crash along with her toddler and husband. That crash occurred only days after an unexpected HR situation sent me to a very dark place. Due to the personal development I have done over the years and my willingness to turn the mirror onto myself each and every time our firm has an issue, I now can look back at that HR situation with gratitude and acceptance of the learning and discoveries that I experienced because of it. Part of that growth is a deep commitment to my own values and aligning our team with those values even if it meant exiting out core-value misaligned team members. This core value, alignment process can be extremely difficult, but it is critical not only to our firm's success but to my emotional well-being.

Certain things I know for sure about my future vision. I will not be the person holding everyone accountable to their measures of success, or KPIs as most owners refer to them. I had a major "aha" moment regarding this role recently. My natural tendency toward accountability falls on the *The Devil Wears Prada* scale; I am hard-driving, I historically work long hours and work on weekends (2400 billable hours per year was 100 percent normal in my past lawyer life), I love efficiency, I manage huge amounts of stress with ease, and I absolutely thrive in change and chaos. Well, let's just say that this "Miranda Priestly" style is not well-suited for today's workforce nor to establishing a firm that is dedicated to a healthy life/work integration. My natural Miranda Priestly tendencies have spurred the decade of learning about leadership, mindset, emotional intelligence, psychology, teams, and trust. But despite that decade of learning and massive self-improvement, my natural "Miranda Priestly" tendencies still live inside me. The emotional turmoil I balance between Miranda's inner voice and my new more enlightened, chill inner voice is not time or emotional energy well-spent. I have an internal battle each time I need to have a tough conversation with a team member, asking myself, "Are your expectations Miranda-like?" "Are you addressing this problem empathetically and with compassion?" The bottom line is that I might be competent in this day-to-day leading gig, but it is not the best use of my time, nor do I enjoy the emotional mind games that Miranda and Eloise play. I'd rather be in the role of CEO—Chief Empowerment

Officer (a.k.a. Firm Cheerleader). In that role, I connect with each of my team members on a regular cadence and encourage them in their dreams and goals both personally and professionally. I don't focus on the day-to-day productivity numbers but instead focus on the alignment of our team, our firm culture, and deepening personal connections. To that end, our firm has a Dream Program where we encourage team members to reach for their BHAG (Big Hairy Audacious Goals) and we commit a quarterly amount of money to a chosen team member's dream. We currently have a team member using her funds to help build her home. I absolutely love fueling other's dreams.

Future visioning requires looking deep inside myself. I do that through daily journaling—making lists like:

- What do I love doing? And why?
- What do I hate doing? And why?
- What mindless things do I do to avoid the harder things?
- What I am great at?
- What do I stink at?
- What is my Number 1 superpower?
- What does a dream day look like?
- What does a dream month look like?
- What does a dream year look like?
- What brings me peace?
- What brings me joy?
- What is soul-crushing?

I have also been reading a wide variety of books, some of whose titles are listed below, which are expanding my thoughts and ideas on what might be next.

The answers to these and other questions will eventually paint a vivid picture of my future and my next vision. Right now, however, it's a blurry brown mess and looks more like a toddler's rendition of potty training. I promised myself and my family that I would spend 2023 focused on my health, my mental well-being, and peace. So as I write this sentence overlooking the snow-capped Olympic Mountains and the Puget Sound with a baby seal on my dock who has a heart-shaped nose, I am struck by how lucky I am to have the time and space to think and dream. I have no great answers about what my future Vision holds except to say that I am deeply committed to disrupting the toxic culture of many law firms. I am also wildly fanatical about the Fair Play method and its potential impact to decrease divorce by bringing substantial equality into homes and to create a solid home-operational system for coparents. I also intend to host gloriously rejuvenating retreats starting in summer 2023 from my beautiful home base in the PNW so that other people can enjoy this extraordinary fjord and the surrounding Olympic National Forest while developing deep personal connections enveloped in warm, Southern hospitality.

Seth Price

If you are choosing the growth path in your legal aspirations, one of the benefits of achieving CEO status is that it gives you an opportunity to focus on your vision. One of my law school professors used to talk about not being able to see the forest through the trees. I didn't fully comprehend what he was talking about until I started running a law firm myself.

Many lawyers accomplish great things in building their firms while practicing law. However, some of the greatest opportunities for growth and systemization in a law firm can only come once a lawyer is given the space and time to truly lead. As a leader's day-to-day operational and legal requirements decrease, they can focus on getting the firm to the next level. Or, as my law professor would put it: they can only focus on the forest when someone else is taking care of the trees.

Once you can look at your law firm from a bird's-eye view, you can make the decisions necessary to get to the next level. If you are stuck pulling weeds, grinding through ongoing obligations every day, you will never reach that point. The transformation comes when the CEO role moves from just a name to an actual position. This opportunity allows you to assess which practice areas are profitable and which need to be tweaked, to reflect and orchestrate the next steps for your firm.

Having the space and time for this kind of mindset can do amazing things for your firm's growth. Allowing the CEO to step away from the office and strategize can pay incredible dividends. Whether you find this space through legal conferences, masterminds, or vacations, the ability to reflect on what works in your absence is a huge step forward. Time away from the office is, in my experience, one of the most valuable resources in flushing out your vision. How is your business running now compared to what you started with? Where do you want to steer your firm in the future? Part of flushing out your vision involves deciding what type of growth you want to pursue. In an ideal world, you would be able to grow across all departments of your firm consistently and evenly. In reality, you need to decide what areas are most important to focus on at any given stage and what areas of growth are next in the pipeline.

When it comes to law firm research and development, I can go overboard in pursuing horizontal growth, especially on the marketing side. I love the idea of diversifying a company; the ups and downs that come with experimenting and taking on different ventures are exciting to me, whether it's social media platforms,

SEO strategies, or different practice groups. However, I recognize the limits of experimentation. At the beginning of a firm's journey, vertical growth may be a wiser plan. Choosing one vertical and staying consistent in that area can significantly benefit your firm. As a simple example, there are plenty of things you can do with a good old-fashioned blog. Consistent, meaningful blog content on your website will resonate with users, drive traffic to your site, and lead to those all-important conversions.

Focused growth within one area is a great way to build upward and outward. On a small scale, a focus on blog content can build your brand's recognition and authority within your community, leading to a long-standing reputation that consistently generates leads for your firm. On a much larger scale, you can build entire practices out of a well-performing department within your firm. I built my law firm, Price Benowitz, with a focus on digital marketing; about five years ago, we took our in-house digital team and created BluShark Digital, which now has a client base of over 100 firms around the country. The merits of having a focused vision within your firm cannot be overstated; sometimes, that focus can spin into new business opportunities and further widen your experience and influence as an entrepreneur and CEO.

In my career, I've been fortunate to work with some amazing people who have been instrumental in building the operation I have today. I wouldn't have been able to get here if I had stayed in the weeds practicing law. There are some people who, through superhuman abilities and lack of sleep, can handle both the chief legal officer and CEO roles. Those people are few and far between; most lawyers will need to step back from their legal duties to create and achieve their visions for their firms.

Give yourself the gift of perspective. Allow yourself to imagine where you want to grow and how you will get there. This ultimate realization of the CEO role can only be accomplished once you have certain fundamentals in place. Your staffing and technology are the building blocks that free you, the founder, to envision the blueprint of what's to come. The CEO role is constantly striving toward a future-oriented ideal. You will certainly deal with many challenges in the present, and it is always good to take stock of where you currently stand. However, you want to get to a place where you have other people taking care of the present. When you can trust your people and your systems to handle the daily issues as they arise, you can set your sights solely on what's ahead.

Reflecting on your firm's past and current stages is undoubtedly helpful in informing your next steps. Still, too many lawyers get stuck in the now, filling their time with small tasks to fix small issues for small returns. Imagining, building, and achieving your vision for the future takes significant time, much of which must be time away from what many lawyers consider work. After many years of daily grinding and focusing solely on your legal career, it may feel like letting your foot off the gas. However, delegating that work to someone else and giving yourself the space to hone your vision is perhaps the greatest thing you can do to move your firm forward.

Ryan McKeen

Vision is the ultimate work of any CEO. Being able to understand where the market is heading and identify opportunities in an ever-changing landscape is the job for any CEO.

There is a lot written on vision in business books. And with good reason. Vision work is very important work. However, I don't think vision work is very difficult at the conceptual level.

Vision work is nothing more and nothing less than knowing where you want to go. It is setting the North Star of your organization.

Doing vision work is a lot like planning a vacation. There is no wrong choice with a vacation. There are just different choices. Choices that are nearly limitless. Certainly a vacation visiting European capitals, hiking the Grand Canyon, surfing in Costa Rica, or going to New York City are all awesome—in very different ways.

Vision is the same. And that's the challenge. Because the question you have to answer is: what do I want? Once you settle on a destination, everything from travel plans to activities to budgeting to what to pack crystallizes.

Any discussion regarding vision begins with what vision actually is. What I outlined above is how I think of vision.

The Power of Vision

Vision begins with setting a ten-year goal. The very best book on the subject is *Traction* by Geno Wickman.

Vision is about setting a ten-year "big hairy audacious goal," and in order to accomplish, that your goal must be all of those things.

In March of 2017, my partner, Andrew Garza, and I set the vision for our firm to be a "10Million Dollar Jury Verdict" by March of 2027. At the time we had only one part-time employee who worked nine hours a week, no cases worth more than 100k, on their best day, no ability to fund a large case, and inadequate systems, training, and technology to support a 10-million-dollar verdict.

We chose that number because our initial impulse was to state that we wanted to be the best personal injury firm in Connecticut. The problem with that is there's no way to determine whether we achieved that vision or not. It was a subjective and standardless goal. Almost like saying our vision for our vacation is that it is awesome.

So we looked around at the top plaintiff's firms in Connecticut and saw that a 10-million-dollar jury verdict would place us in the discussion as best personal injury firm in Connecticut. So we wrote that down as our vision, and I'm glad we did.

Just over five years later, we would have a team of thirty people, the ability to spend into cases, systems, highly trained trial lawyers, and best-in-class tech to achieve a 100-million-dollar jury verdict.

I will spare you the details in this chapter, but setting that vision was the choice that made a 100-million-dollar jury verdict possible.

More Vision Work

This, of course, leads me to where I am now at the time of this writing (February 2023), which is redoing our vision work. We need another big hairy audacious goal. And I'm working on it.

This time, I'm involving everyone. I'm talking 1:1 for a half hour at a minimum on the topic of vision with everyone on my team. I'm asking them questions about who we are, what is important, where they want to go, and what would make them proud of working at our firm.

I don't know what our vision will end up being. I do know that this process has been incredibly valuable. And I'm certain our vision will be better and we will have more buy-in because we've involved team members early in the process.

This brings up another point, which is that vision work is ongoing. You should be asking yourself at your early meetings if your vision is still the right one for your team. And when you get to where you want to go, it is time to plan another trip.

Vision for the Future of the Profession

When I think about the future of the profession, all I see is massive change. The legal profession will change more in the next ten years than it has in the last two hundred by orders of magnitude.

On the Micro Level

The exact changes, when they will occur, and what their impacts will be are incredibly hard to predict. Change will be uneven. It will not be linear, and it will be more influenced by changes outside of the profession than in it.

On The Macro Level

Large pools of money are looking to extract profits from legal. In 2023, no one firm has more even 1 percent market share in the legal industry. This at a time when consolidation is king. Outside of the legal industry, companies are larger than ever. Every day, bigger fish gobble up smaller fish in every market. This, of course, results in less competition, more efficiency, and greater returns to shareholders. There is no reason to think legal will be immune from these larger market forces.

This will happen when deregulation happens, which is already underway. The combination of big money, changing demographics leaving bar associations less powerful politically, and societal needs make this a question of *when* and not *if* in every state.

In the meantime, you will see consolidation on the sidelines. You will see consolidation in legal marketing, where some players become dominant and sell leads to those who deliver services. You will see continued maturation of the legal finance space where lines of credit and case funding become ubiquitous players in all markets in an effort to grab a slice of the pie.

On the delivery side, what passes for legal tech today will look quaint in the next ten years. Legal tech won't be about tasking—it will function as your back office, operations, and paralegal staff. It will do input, extraction, and processing of information for you.

So What Should You Do?

Focus on work that can't be automated. If it can be done by a robot, it will be done by a robot. The AI technology is here now and is about to get a lot better. Get your systems, data, and processes in order now. General machine learning is one level, but the next level is it learning your specific systems—the difference between a chainsaw and a scalpel.

Future legal service providers will be free from the mundane. And those with the ability to do it will focus their work on the important.

Focus on branding. If people know you and search for your name, you will stand a chance against larger marketers that will move into your market.

Finally, focus on being human. Great people helping other people, doing tasks that involve judgment and connection are going nowhere. Go out there and build your community. Get out of your office and find lawyers, paralegals, and business professionals who are amazing at what they do and even better people.

The future of law is human. And I couldn't be more optimistic about that.

Jay Ruane

Now that I have put myself in the position of CEO, I have a new vision—replace myself as CEO and be 100 percent OUT. This is a huge step for me; I never thought this would be my endgame until recently. The reality of building a firm that can function without me is that I should be exiting to do something else. Sure, that something else could be building a new firm or a new business, but I am starting to think that it will look much different from that.

Looking back now at this twenty-five year journey, I sacrificed a lot. I was broke, saddled with debt, and hustling when my friends had gotten well-paying jobs that afforded them paid vacation. They traveled, they started families. For me, that was not the path. I spent many weekend nights working ON the business, learning the skills to do things more cheaply than I could buy on the market because I was short on funds but long on time. I'm not as long on time anymore, and I'm starting to think that my next iteration doesn't include traditional business. I've started a group coaching business that focuses on my people, only criminal defense lawyers, and it is fun and flourishing. I find myself drawn to the things needed to keep giving value to that group, mainly because I didn't have anything like that when I started. Hell, I didn't have anything like that even 10 years ago.

But if I want to really step away, I need to confirm that my time inside law was coming to an end, and that is still a hard decision to accept. If you have read *Tiger Tactics 1*, there are a lot of familial reasons why I chose my practice area and built the firm I did. Looking forward, I am ready to step out, but my father still isn't. I would be leaving him behind, and that is a BIG deal to me. Even writing this chapter has been therapeutic in a way because these are feelings I have had for a while now but have never expressed out loud, let alone to anyone else. Now I am sharing it with the great community out there of legal entrepreneurs, and maybe, just maybe, that means I need to exit that community as well. I am not sure, but I do know that in order to define my pathway forward, I need to make absolutely sure I am done with each step of the process—working in law, working on law business, and then working out of law. So I've taken some time recently to work at each level to make sure I am making the right decisions.

Working in law: A criminal defense lawyer is a daily grinder. We are at court every day, hustling in hallways, taking calls at night, and working on the craft of being a lawyer. In order to do this job well, you need to know more about the science you are fighting than anyone else in the courtroom, and that means going to seminars and learn from the best. I'm lucky; over the time at practice I've built some deep friendships with the best in the subject matters I encounter, and I can turn to them if I need help. But recently, when I attended a DUI seminar, I was blown away by the younger lawyers in the room. Pushing hard for verdicts and to get the right deal for their client. Learning way more complicated concepts than I have even encountered, and just inspiring me with their passion and energy. Even hitting courthouses over the last six months to cover cases, I have seen some amazing young lawyers doing their thing. I've gotten some really good results for my clients along the way too, mind you, but I have definitely concluded that my time at courthouses grinding away is done. Like Marie Kondo has said about cleaning up— being at a courthouse doesn't "spark joy" for me anymore. I might find a flash of inspiration or some joy in a particular case result for a deserving client, but I know after self-reflection that it's time to step away.

Working in the business of law: This has been my passion for twenty-plus years, and I will always be involved in some degree with helping others run their law business better. That's one of the reasons I created the Law Firm Blueprint show/podcast/group. I know what it is like to try to do this alone, and I hated the feeling of being alone. I want to be a giver and help people avoid all the issues I came across in my journey. Helping people, whether my clients or other lawyers, was always at the core of my identity. I have always been a giver, and this is a way to be the best version of myself. It's one reason I agreed to *Tiger Tactics 1* and then pushed for *Tiger Tactics 2*. Law can be a thrilling, exhilarating, and wonderfully rewarding career, but it can also be lonely and exhausting, and you can spend YEARS in between those milestones that bring joy. I want people to know that you should find joy in the small victories, like converting a single new client from your email campaign, even more than dollar-sign revenue goals.

Working out of law: As we come to the end of this book and my own career in law, I am truly proud of what I built. You always hear "they didn't teach us this in law school" from other lawyers, and while that may be true, they also didn't stop you from teaching it to yourself or studying those who have done it. That's the reality—anything worth having is worth pursuing, and sometimes you just need to embark on your own path and not be held back by others (or yourself). Yes, it includes risk.

My path forward will end with me owning a fully capable, fully independent law firm. I will be a CE-OUT, much like an investor owns an apartment building or any other functional business. It can market itself, service the clientele, heal itself with the systems we have put in place, and continue to grow and provide for me while I embark on the next part of this journey without the law firm as part of my daily experience. I can't wait for the next few years because I have learned so much in the last twenty-five that I didn't have going into this. Coming out, I am a tremendously different person and can do so much more. Look out, you aren't done with me yet, because I'm not done with me yet either.

CONCLUSION

As you have read throughout this book, the pathway to Lawyer CEO is individualized and unique to your journey, but like any explorer, you can lean on others who have done similar journeys to help you know how to prepare, what you are facing, and what tools to bring.

It is not for us to dictate your way. You alone get to set your destination. And while the journey will have both ups and downs, we wish nothing else for you but to experience and live through each one of them, as we have and will continue to do so as we take our own path to CEO.

Please, reach out to us as you grow from Zero to Law Firm CEO. We are your biggest supporters and can't wait to see the amazing things you will show the world.

Jay Ruane

Ryan McKeen

Billie Tarascio

William Umansky

Elise Buie

Jennifer Gore-Cuthbert

Sandy Van

Michelle Dellino

Joey Vitale

Mario A. Godoy

Allison McKeen

Allison C. Williams

Seth J. Price

RESOURCES:

Ryan McKeen
- Scaling Up: Mastering the Rockefellers written by Verne Harnish

Jay Ruane
- Hugh MacLeod, British artist.
- Get Staffed Up - VA company - https://getstaffedup.com/

Billie Tarascio
- Win Without Law School winwithoutlawschool.com
- Culture Amp - https://www.cultureamp.com
- Criteria Corp - https://www.criteriacorp.com/
- Trainual - https://trainual.com/

Elise Buie
- Fireproof written by Michael Morse and John Nachazel
- Profit First written by Michael Michalowicz
- The New One Minute Manager written by Ken Blanchard
- Upleveling Your Business. Tell Kristen I sent you and ask for a VIP Discount!

Sandy Van
- Who Not How: The Formula to Achieve Bigger Goals Through Accelerating Teamwork written by Dan Sullivan and Dr. Benjamin Hardy
- Darren Hardy, editor of Success Magazine.
- Legal Support Help, my virtual assistant staffing company
- Snowball written by Warren Buffet.

- Jarrett Prussin -https://businessfundinggroup.com/meet-the-team/
- Jeff Huff or Ronnie Watkins
  - https://alfcapital.com/author/jhuff/
- Network organizations: Entrepreneurs' Organization (EO) and the Young Presidents' Organization (YPO).
- Who: The A Method for Hiring written by Geoff Smart
- Reports - https://legalprintables.com/
- Law Firm Success - coaching company for attorneys.

Mario Godoy

- RJon Robins - Business Consultant - https://rjonrobins.com/
- Kristen David of Upleveling Your Business
- E-Myth by Michael Gerber
- Good to Great: Why Some Companies Make the Leap and Others Don't written by Jim Collins
- Onboarding system
  - https://godoylawoffice.com/onboarding.
- Jack Welch
- David Emeril's on The Power of TED
- Scaling Up: Mastering the Rockefellers written by Verne Harnish

Jenn Gore-Cuthbert

- "Fireproof" by Michael Morse and John Nachazel

Bill Umansky

- Strategic Coach is an entrepreneurial coaching company. https://www.strategiccoach.com/
- The 4 C's Formula written by Dan Sullivan

Joey Vitale

- For an Elevator Chart template send an email to joey@indielaw.com.

- Vivid Vision: A Remarkable Tool For Aligning Your Business Around a Shared Vision of the Future written by Cameron Herold
- Velocity Work www.velocitywork.com
- Christopher White - www.eques.law

Allison Williams

- Real Talent Hiring assessment — an extensive assessment tool that tells you information about how a candidate manages tasks, themselves, and others.
- Relentless Solution Focus written by Dr. Jason Selk
- Claire Parsons' Brilliant Legal Minds guided meditations
- Who Not How written by Dan Sullivan